Zero Ward

A Survivor's Nightmare

Lived & Written
by
Murray M. Sneddon, P.O.W.

Writers Club Press
San Jose · New York · Lincoln · Shanghai

Dedication

This story was lived and written by Murray M. Sneddon. Before he could finish it he died of leukemia. He began the book in 1985 at the suggestion and encouragement of family and friends, so it is dedicated to them: Laurie Reber, Wendy Duncan and Tom Sneddon, daughters and son. Originally his father, Richard Sneddon, suggested he write this story and his sister, Delta Murphy, also thought it should be published.

Friends and fellow survivors: Diane & Brad Mettam, computer wizards without whose help it would not have been published; Paul Young, a teacher and writer who researched and added the section on Cabanatuan which Murray had not completed; survivors Rev. John Morrett and Carl Nordin, who wrote their own stories and encouraged Murray. Of course there are others too numerous to mention, such as friends in Burbank and Bishop.

The art work was originally created for three issues of the 1945 Colliers magazines. Some of them have been used with Murray's permission in other books, namely "Soldier Priest."

Contents

List of Photos and Drawings

Letters From War Department

Newspaper Articles

Miscellaneous

Chapter 1

The Beginning of
the End (Prologue)

The story I'm about to tell you really began to come to a close one hot August night in the year 1944. Six hundred and fifty of us, all American prisoners of war, were working on the island of Mindanao in the southern Philippines.

About six months prior to this day the Japanese sent us from the main prison camp near Davao City, a camp holding about 2,000 men, to work on a new military airfield on the outskirts of the village of Lasang. The Lasang villagers dared not approach our prison compound on threat of death. So, although we were held captive in their country, we never saw them.

The fact that the Japanese forced us to work on one of their airfields rankled our souls like a festering ulcer. The anger generated by this witless affront to our national honor almost became our undoing. We complained bitterly to our leaders; they in turn complained to the Japs.

Our commanders reminded them of the Geneva Conference on the Rules of Land Warfare which most of the world's civilized nations had signed. They reminded us that they had not signed the aforementioned documents and would do with us what they pleased. If we did not do the work they requested, we would be killed. This was no idle threat. We had ample proof from the past that they were quite capable of following through on such an assertion.

As a result of this ultimatum, not only were we working on a military project which gave assistance to the enemies of our country, a bitter pill for us to swallow, but our only recourse was to drag our feet as much as possible while giving the impression we were hard at work. A dangerous game to play! One that could end in tragedy.

While we worked in extreme heat without hats or other essential clothing to protect us from the sun, the Nips turned a deaf ear to all our complaints and ordered us to level the ground adjacent to the runway with picks and shovels and

1

to widen the landing strip. We had to pack the new surface with coral and sometimes were ordered to leave the job momentarily to rescue aircraft that strayed too close to the edge of the runway and became bogged down in the mud.

This behavior was unbelievable, for many of us were pilots and others were from air base groups who had worked on planes during their entire military careers. We naively took a firm hold on the vertical stabilizer, elevators, an aileron or pilot tube, or some other equally vital structure while the Japs ran crazily among us cursing the stupid Americans who didn't have more sense than to lift a plane by its control surfaces. There were several crashes on take-off and we fervently hoped that our attempts at sabotage had been at least partially responsible.

The extreme heat and humidity on the airfield robbed us of every last vestige of strength. That, and the totally inadequate diet we were fed, left us perpetually without energy. Davao lay only six degrees above the equator, the sun's fiery heat shimmering up from the vast expanse of a white coral runway made even breathing an effort.

We had returned from the airfield that afternoon, staggering in a ragged column of fours over a heavily graveled road that raised havoc with our tender bare feet. We were not permitted to wear shoes because the Japs thought they enhanced our chances for escape. As we neared the gate of the compound, we straightened our ranks so we could be counted back in—a regimen imposed by the Japanese to ensure none of us had escaped. As each four men passed through the gate and were counted, they broke ranks and ran to be the early ones to get to what we jokingly called our shower. The shower consisted of pouring two or three buckets of muddy well water over our heads and rubbing vigorously to be rid of the sweat and grime that had accumulated after a grueling day on the airfield. We had no soap. We had been prisoners now for almost two and a half years and had never been given a bar of soap to properly cleanse ourselves. We had no towels, although they really weren't necessary in the tropics. The days were so humid that the water drying on our bodies left us momentarily cool and refreshed.

As it grew close to suppertime, we prepared to draw our meager ration of boiled rice, which was standard fare for breakfast, and lunch also. The Japs brought us our allotment of food daily. The rice was cooked in large cast-iron bowls called *kawas*. Our cooks cooked it; our servers served it. As we passed through the line the server plunged a stick with a flat oval-shaped empty fish can nailed to it into the *kawa* of rice. With a stick in his other hand he raked across the top of the can, thus leveling the contents. The portion measured a little over seven ounces of cooked rice. For the most part that was the extent of each meal. On some occasions during the appropriate seasons we received some *camote*, a Philippine sweet potato. In many instances, however, a rotten *camote* inadvertently wound up in the pot with the good ones and when all were mashed to ensure equitable servings, the whole mess was so foul it couldn't be eaten. On one or two occasions we received a total of two fish for the 650 of us. Although it was possible to pick up the flavor of the fish in the rice, the flesh of the fish itself could not be detected.

The portion we received for each meal was woefully inadequate in both size and nutritional value to sustain men who were required to do heavy work. We had all wasted away considerably from our normal weights. I had a chance to weigh myself on a rice scale one day. It was set to 90 pounds, the minimum acceptable weight for a sack of rice. When I stepped on the platform of the scale, the pointer failed to move up. I knew then that I weighed less than 90 pounds but I didn't know how much less. My normal weight was 150 pounds.

After eating, we cleaned up our mess kits and began to prepare for the evening, which was a time to sit and think about our situation. Usually some men stayed outside the barracks studying the constellations and tried desperately to remove themselves mentally from this place. Others went inside and sat down to talk. On this particular evening I returned to my barracks to sit and talk with my friends.

The barracks were long and narrow and housed 165 men each. They were divided down the middle by an aisle. One-third of the distance from each end was a cross aisle, dividing the barracks into six bays. There were no floors in the buildings, just dirt, as each barrack rested right on the ground. About 14 inches above ground there was a sleeping platform of solid wood. I was sitting on the edge of this platform with my feet on the ground.

At 9:00 o'clock the lights were turned out and we began to move back onto our platforms to sleep for the night. For a while a few voices still buzzed in the distance, but gradually the talking trailed off and in a little while all became quiet.

As I lay there I heard a small, weak, droning sound. At first I wasn't sure whether it came from some insect within the building or its source was beyond the prison compound. It sounded vaguely familiar, but I couldn't identify it with any certainty. For a moment it subsided, but then it came back again. As I lay there listening, the sound got increasingly louder. I became aware that nobody in the building was moving. Everyone was still. Everyone was listening. Soon it was directly above us, moving in a lazy circle. Then we heard the sound of objects rushing down through the air, and bombs bursting at the airfield we had left only a few hours ago.

My heart raced with excitement. I couldn't believe that after two-and-a-half years of imprisonment our forces were suddenly able to reach us. The compound lights were turned off outside. We could hear the guards yelling back and forth. We heard them running in their heavy hobnailed boots, and in a very few moments they had encircled every barrack, weapons held at the ready. The situation was tense; it was not time to talk or to move. We remained motionless but our minds were racing.

I had a difficult time sleeping that night. I remember wondering what this sudden turn of events might mean. How long would it be before any of us might have a chance for freedom? Thoughts of home flooded over me: my parents, my girlfriend Fee. I wanted so desperately to get back home. Yet there was no way of divining what still lay ahead. The next morning, to the great surprise of the Japanese, we approached the gate ready to go to work ahead of schedule. We were extremely anxious to find out what had happened up there at the airfield. We wanted to assess the damage with our own eyes, and see what revenge the planes had wrought. But there was some confusion, some kind of delay at the gate. We waited but nothing happened to give us any information.

The next morning we came back bright and early again. Frustrated again, we stayed in camp another day.

The third day we were told to get our belongings. Well, this took me only about two seconds. All I had was a single blanket and a mess kit. I just rolled them up and returned to the gate ready to go. Tragically, there was no clue what was about to happen to us on the rest of our journey.

The 17th of August, 1944 dawned clear and hot. Before noon the heat climbed to the uncomfortable stage. Massive cumulus clouds over the distant mountains pushed their way up to 30,000 feet or more. By 2:00 in the afternoon anvil-shaped thunderclouds leveled off the tallest cloud columns and soon small villages along the base of the mountains were deluged with a torrent of rain. The rampant waters inundated the land, but the tall bamboo stilts that supported the village dwellings kept them dry and safe. The rain pummeled the area for an hour or two; then, as if by heavenly command, stopped as quickly as it had started.

Seasons seem to dictate the weather patterns in the northern islands. Dry periods and wet periods alternate according to the months of the year, but here in southern Mindanao, only six degrees above the equator, the seasonal activities of the north are squeezed into one day. But the daily release of all these compressed energies is considered quite normal for this section of the Philippines. Tragically, the weather failed to present us with any clue that this day would vary from the norm. There was not a hint that something cataclysmic was about to happen.

Chapter 2

Before World War II

I arrived in California when I was just four years old, brought from Winnipeg, Manitoba, Canada where I was born. My father was born in Wishaw, Scotland, a suburb of Glasgow. My mother, like me was Canadian, born in Varna, Ontario. My sister, Delta, six years younger than me was born in Long Beach, California two years after my parents and I arrived in the United States. I have always enjoyed teasing her by referring to her as the only foreigner in our family.

I attended Kindergarten at Fries Avenue Grammar School in Wilmington, California. My father's employer, the Union Oil Co. of California, then transferred him to a new site and I finished my elementary training at Miles Avenue Elementary School in Huntington Park. I attended Gage Avenue Junior High through the first half of the eighth grade, then once again our family moved, this time to Glendale where I finished junior high and all my high school education at Hoover High School. I enjoyed athletics but couldn't compete on the "A" level; I was too small and light. Tennis was my best sport but I also lettered in Class "C" Basketball and Football. I did not participate much in social activities. I was quite shy, and rather terrified of girls, primarily because I had not learned to dance.

As graduation time grew nearer I decided I wanted to attend college. My school counselors helped me plan my program so that I might qualify for entrance to UCLA. Of course, it depended on how diligent I was in working for good grades. I really worked very hard my last year and finished my last semester with all A's. One of my art teachers informed me that she felt I could get a scholarship to Chouinard Art School. This excited me greatly because art had always been my favorite subject and I really wanted to be trained as an artist. This did not meet with my parents' approval, however. They wanted me to get a degree from a university. They were not particularly interested in the subject field I chose, as long as I obtained the degree. They indicated that it was perfectly acceptable to them if I obtained my degree in art. They were willing to provide me with all the necessary funds to complete my college education, so I felt obligated to do as they asked. Nonetheless, I was bitterly disappointed in having to follow a course for my life with which I was not in sympathy.

I had talked to students who had attended Chouinard and Art Center schools who said that a degree gave no proof of your ability in your job field, whereas the high degree of skill attained by a graduating student of our best art schools was evident in his personal portfolio and in his daily work.

I entered UCLA and continued in the study of art for two and one-half years. I continued to be depressed by the lack of skill I was acquiring. I talked with counselors in the art department and was informed that I would not be able to receive training comparable to that received by a commercial artist, and that the goal of the college was to train art teachers. That was not my goal. I couldn't understand, too, why any art student would want to receive instruction from someone who could only talk about art and not demonstrate the skill the student wished to acquire.

Each day on my route to college I passed the Glendale Air Terminal and saw young men my age receiving flight training. At times I parked my car and watched for a while before heading home. In my depressed state this really looked exciting to me and I began thinking about it more and more. Soon I decided I was wasting precious time on the way to a career and decided to drop out of college. I needed time to think and plan what I should do next. After leaving UCLA, I thought a good deal more about flight training and finally dropped by the Army Air Corps office at the terminal building.

When I left the office I was even more positive about pursuing that course of action. I would be paid monthly while in training at a salary which seemed enormous to me. I would be furnished with all necessities: uniforms, books, meals and lodging, at no cost to me. Upon graduating I would be presented my silver wings and would be commissioned as a Second Lieutenant. A permanent job awaited me with an established squadron where I could advance my skill. Who could ask for more! All of this lovely dream, however, depended on two important prerequisites. First, I must pass the physical examination. It was thorough and demanded a high level of perfection as well as taking a whole day to complete. Second, because I was born in Canada, I was required to submit proof of American citizenship. I decided not to worry about the second part since my parents had spent several years going to night school to acquire their citizenship papers. As I was still a minor, I was considered a citizen because of their status.

Obviously the first step was to take the physical exam. If I failed it, I could forget about the citizenship requirement and I would have to give up all hope of becoming a military pilot. However, by the time I graduated from flight training I would no longer be a minor. At that time I would have to make a choice. I could accept the American citizenship my parents had acquired for me, or I could retain the citizenship of my birth.

2nd Observation Squadron—Clark Field, Philippine Islands. June 24, 1941

I obtained the form required to take the physical. Unfortunately I discovered another prerequisite even more threatening than the previous two. Since I was a minor I would have to get my parents' permission to enter the program. I had to face this new hurdle right away so I requested a talk with my parents. They were already very unhappy about my leaving college. To make matters worse, my mother was terrified of airplanes and steadfastly swore never to set foot in one so long as she lived. She was certain that of all planes that successfully became airborne, only a handful managed to land successfully. The others crashed with great loss of life.

I was very careful to talk calmly, positively, and with sincerity and conviction. To my complete astonishment they agreed to sign my paper giving their permission to my venture. I made sure they understood that if I failed the physical exam I could not proceed further. Perhaps that was what clinched it.

I received my appointment to take the physical exam but was surprised to note that the date was almost two months away. I decided to use the time to better prepare myself for the ordeal ahead. I was aware that the many eye tests were the greatest eliminators of candidates taking the exam, so I embarked on a vigorous program of self-denial which I felt would improve my visual performance. Movies were out! They placed too much strain on the eyes. Likewise reading— for the same reason. To deny both these pastimes was most difficult. I dearly loved them both. But in my mind, to set them both aside for a time was quite necessary. I ran around the block—it was a long one—at top speed. I did push-ups every evening and anytime I thought of exercising. I retired early each night. I did everything that I reasoned would improve my health and better my chances of passing.

On the day of the exam I walked into the office about fifteen minutes ahead of time. For a short period of time I was alone, but soon three other young men about my own age arrived and we all sat in the waiting room together. None of us spoke. I think each one of us was deep in his own thoughts trying to mentally prepare for what was ahead. Soon we were given long and rather complicated questionnaires to complete. Then each of us was sent to a different area to begin various tests and interviews. Just before noon, one of our number dejectedly bid us goodbye and went out the exit from the building. This began to raise my level of stress until I realized that worry was the last thing I needed to bring me through this ordeal. I settled down.

I quickly learned why the eye tests were so devastating in their effect on applicants. I had never realized how many ways the eyes could be tested. I peered through holes in an armor-like mask that was placed against my face. I followed lights in the dark that roamed up and down, back and forth, split apart and rejoined. I was handed two heavy cords that entered a white box some 10 or 15 feet in front of me. Through a window in the front of that box I could see two dark vertical rods, one of which could be moved by pulling one or the other of the two cords. The operator conducting the test adjusted the moveable rod either in front or behind the stationary rod, then asked me to adjust the cords so that both rods were side by side. After complying with his requests a number of times I was sent back to the gentleman with the iron mask again. He put drops in my eyes that stung quite a bit at first, but later settled down. After a short period of time he turned off the light and searched the interior parts of my eyes with a small flashlight that nearly blinded me. Then away we went again. "Look up. Look down. Follow this light! Tell me when both lights come together." I felt certain that when this exam was over I would never see again. I was sent back to the waiting room to rest a moment before the next ordeal. There I learned that both of the remaining applicants had been sent home. I was the only one left. When I left the Air Corps Training Office in the Airport Terminal Building, I felt more positive than ever about pursuing the Cadet Flight Training Program. Although I knew my parents were going to be very unhappy that I was dropping out of college, the school counselors—after two and one-half years—finally confessed to me that they didn't have a course of study leading to a degree in Commercial Illustration.

Chapter 3

The
Other Side
of the World

I arrived in the Philippines on board the SS Washington on May 8, 1941. The ship docked at the Cavite Naval Yards on Manila Bay and shortly after we disembarked, those of us who were members of the Army Air Corps were flown to Clark Field, 50 miles north of Manila. There I was assigned as a reconnaissance pilot with the 2nd Observation Squadron flying single-engine Thomas Morris biplanes.

Although the threat of war with Japan was in the air, the squadrons operating in the Philippines were equipped with older, slower planes than were those squadrons in the States. Many of our pursuit planes plodded along anywhere from 100 to 150 mph slower than the new planes coming off the assembly lines at home. And they were certainly slower than the Japanese fighters.

My job in the 2nd Observation Squadron was to fly photo reconnaissance over many of the neighboring islands and to monitor shipping in the waters around Luzon, the northernmost and largest island in the Philippine Archipelago. For the most part, it was tedious work and at no time did I spot any activity on the part of the Japanese.

On the 26th of October I was transferred to Nichols Field 20 miles to the north of Manila, and remained there until the beginning of the war. And although I logged in many flying hours out of Nichols, the work was again tedious.

I did see a great deal of the Philippines from the air and met many of the Filipino people wherever I landed. During that time I grew very fond of both the place and the people who inhabited the islands.

As the month of November came to an end, the relationship between America and Japan was rapidly deteriorating and most of us felt that war was imminent. Yet we were not gearing up for war as diligently as many of us thought we should be. Some 30 new P-40 pursuit planes had arrived earlier at Nichols Field, but sat for three months waiting for a shipment of coolant so the engines could be flown. Most of our bomber and fighter planes were no match for the Japanese, and Command seemed reluctant to act without orders from higher up the chain of command.

So we waited.

It was on December 8, 1941, while I was at Nichols Field, when news reached us that Pearl Harbor had been bombed. The initial plan was to disperse the planes throughout the area when war started to prevent their sudden and complete destruction. When we arrived at the ready room, expecting those orders, we were told to wait until word came from higher authority.

And there we waited.

Finally, at the end of the day, when so simple an instruction as to disperse the planes off the runway failed to come, and our immediate Command failed to take the initiative and issue those orders, we were told to return to our billets for the night.

I was in my bunk during the early hours of the morning when I was awakened by the tremendous roar of airplanes immediately overhead. Then the bombs began to fall, bursting with deafening explosions over the airfield. I grabbed my clothes, pulling them on as I ran from my hut into a world on fire. Hangers were burning, planes were burning, men screaming and hollering in the chaos around us. I leapt into a trench as the Japanese continued to bomb and strafe the airfield, and there I stayed through what up until that moment was the most terrifying time in my life. Huddled in the trench, it seemed as though the bombing would never end.

By morning my plane, like almost every plane on the field, was a blackened engine sitting in a pile of ashes and twisted aluminum. As an aerial fighting force, we had ceased to exist.

By day's end we had laid out over 150 dead and tended to more than 75 wounded, some of whom would later die.

After the wounded were sent off to hospitals and the dead buried, what was left of the squadron set up operations in a grove of trees bordering what had once been our runway, but was now heavily cratered by bombs.

And there we stayed until Christmas Day, when we were ordered to report to the docks near Manila. From there we went by inter-island steamer to the southern end of the Bataan Peninsula. On Bataan, since we had no planes to fly, we were assigned to a reserve infantry unit. Eventually we became coastal observers, watching for an attempt by the enemy to land behind our main line of defense further up the peninsula.

Chapter 4

The Death March

There is probably no phase of the World War II Philippine campaign that attracts more attention than the Death March. Those three words seem to act like a magnet. People are drawn to a recitation of all the atrocities attributed to that part of the campaign before they know much else about the factors that brought about the atrocities, and what effect atrocities had on the men who became POWs. Furthermore, a simple analysis of that event will help you to see why the title, the Death March, really doesn't accurately describe what happened.

Manila Bay is a huge body of water. It can hold and protect a whole fleet of ships. This is possible because the bay is shaped roughly like an enclosed triangle. The top leg of the triangle is made up primarily of the city of Manila and its suburbs. The right leg is made up entirely of the large Cavite Naval Base. Bataan Peninsula encloses the left-hand side of the Bay.

Where Bataan Peninsula and Cavite meet there is a small opening. In the center of that opening rests the fortified island of Corregidor, The Rock. There are gigantic guns on Corregidor, but unfortunately for the men of Bataan those gigantic guns are fixed in position so they can fire only out to sea. Think how the outcome of the Battle of Bataan might have changed if those guns could have been reversed.

No foreign power can claim to have possession of the Philippines unless it controls Corregidor. Only the island of Corregidor can prevent or allow the passage of ships into the Bay. The Bataan Peninsula runs almost due north. Its central section is occupied by mountains. A dirt road runs around the edge of the peninsula except for a segment of some ten or fifteen miles on the northwest coast, between Morong and Olongapo. The mountains are covered with dense

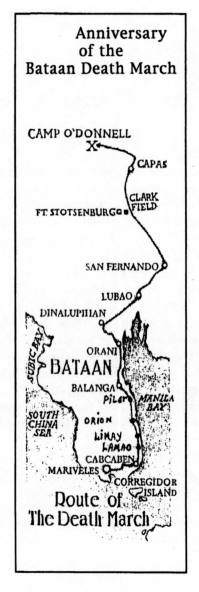

EX-POW BULLETIN, APRIL 1996

Map of the Death March

forests except for a few level sections on which the natives grow rice. For the most part, the area between the road and the shore also supports heavy tree growth. The soldiers of Bataan occupied most of the forested areas where good concealment was available.

Our Bataan force did well for four months. Then two things happened. First, when Singapore fell, the Japanese were able to move into Bataan some of their most experienced troops, who had been fighting in China and Indonesia for years. Second, the Bataan force was running out of both food and ammunition; many men had become ill.

Apparently General Homma's new army was superior to the first because he was now able to force the surrender of Bataan. On April 9, 1942, General King decided he could no longer continue the fight so, after notifying General MacArthur, he surrendered the entire Bataan Force to General Homma. Naturally, General Homma wanted Corregidor surrendered as well, but General King could not surrender that which was not under his command. So Homma, who had been unable to defeat the Bataan force before, was now eager, with his new army, to bring about the surrender of Corregidor, Japan's last barrier to full possession and control of all the Philippine Islands.

The Japanese newspapers and radio had not been kind to Homma, and had held him up for ridicule because he had been unable to defeat a greatly inferior Bataan force. Homma was ready to restore his dignity no matter what the cost.

When General Homma felt sure of his defeat of the Bataan forces, he called his staff together to plan the last step in the Philippine Campaign, the assault on Corregidor. He realized first he must move all American soldiers out of Bataan as quickly as possible, while, at the same time, he moved his own forces in to assault Corregidor.

He decided the American captives should be marched out as far as the city of San Fernando. From there they would be transported by railroad to Capas. Then another march to Camp O'Donnell, our first prison camp. Unfortunately things did not turn out to be quite as simple as the plan indicated. This was due to some serious blunders on the part of the Japanese.

The Japanese estimated the size of the American forces to be around 50,000, whereas the actual number was closer to 75,000. American commanders were shocked to learn that our rations were dwindling fast, so our troops were put on half- rations. This resulted in much illness. The Japanese assumed all troops were healthy and well, so no accommodation for the sick and wounded was planned along the route of the march. The most drastic lack of consideration was given to the greatest problem that faced us. What would the attitude of the Japanese guards be toward the American captives?

To implement their plan the Japanese sent foot soldiers into Bataan starting at the north end of the peninsula. They entered American bivouac areas and moved all POWs out to the road, then headed them north with a small escort of guards. They continued with that pattern, moving as fast as possible toward the southern end of the peninsula. I was attached to Air Corps Headquarters. Our bivouac area was well around the end of the peninsula. By the time the Japanese reached us, more than a week had passed since the surrender. From our distant location it took us more than ten days to finish the march.

So it's important to understand the Death March varied in length according to the distance south the soldiers were bivouacked. Some POWs completed the march in as little as two days, while others required ten or more.

I remember well my introduction to the Death March. A single Japanese soldier came into my area and pointed toward the road. I understood what he was indicating. I stood up, put my pack over my shoulder, and started walking. I had very carefully examined the articles in my pack and in my wallet. I destroyed everything that referred to anything more than my name, rank, or serial number. My canteen was filled with cold clear water. I thought I was ready.

When I arrived at the road I got a terrible shock. There in front of me lay two corpses, both Americans. Their bodies were burned black by the heat from the Philippine sun. The gases generated by decay had blown up both bodies to almost twice normal size. The skin had stretched far beyond its capacity, revealing through tears parts of the skeleton within. Maggots in limitless numbers wriggled and crawled over every opening in the skin, making the bodies seem almost alive. Swarms of flies with luminous blue bodies hovered just above the corpses and the angry drone of their flight made the whole scene even more eerie. Then, as my wide circuit around the bodies reached the downwind side, I suddenly caught the horrible stench of death and I quickly clapped my hand over my nose and mouth to keep from vomiting on the spot.

I quickly diverted my gaze from the horror before me and I asked God to bless both men. I particularly gave thanks to God that their loved ones would never see them as I had seen them.

I was aroused from my preoccupation by a low guttural growl from one of the Japanese soldiers. He was standing with his legs wide apart, hands grasping his rifle, and he gestured with his bayonet. As I turned and looked at him I understood very clearly that he wanted me to move and move fast into the end of the forming column. Not wanting to be a part of another death scene, I quickly joined the column.

As we began to march along the road, I realized how fortunate I had been to rest for a week away from the brutal aspects of war; protected from the incessant heat, free of the demands of men, and enchanted by the beauties of the forests of Bataan. Now things were slowly reversing. The Japanese were in charge, and we were well aware that the war had returned.

Even more critical was the return of the sun. We had left the cool of the forests and were now at the mercy of that ever-present fiery ball in the sky. Our road was deep with dust and as our energy waned, our gait changed from a walking one to a shuffling one. This kicked up the dust and kept us surrounded with foul air which was difficult to breathe.

Those who were ill when we started faced a terrible dilemma which we soon experienced. As we trudged along, each man deep in his own thoughts, the sharp crack of a rifle suddenly shattered the air. Needless to say, we marchers were really startled. A few men turned and looked back but quickly faced forward again and warned others to keep moving. This was a forced march we were making. Any man who could not keep up the pace, and as a result fell behind the column, was finished. One of the guards who brought up the rear of the column simply placed the muzzle of his rifle against the skull of the faltering POW and pulled the trigger. The prisoner fell immediately into a crumpled heap and the guard stepped over the body and looked for possible new candidates ahead. This was not an isolated incident. Many more of these executions occurred before the day's march was over. From the very first time I sighted a Japanese soldier to the final day of the Death March, I never saw one of them smile, nor did I see them joking or talking together. They were all sullen and mean-looking. They had been given no order covering treatment of the sick, so they handled it in the easiest way. They simply killed them all.

Since the moment one of our members was executed at the rear of the column, a great change had come over our group. The marching pace increased, no man spoke, and every man realized this was no weekend outing. Any one of us could be killed instantly. This was a life and death matter. The guards were capable of annihilating all of us for little or no reason. We had to be as serious in our intent as the Japanese were in theirs. We became wary and watchful.

Later in the afternoon of that first day our guards led us beyond the side of the road into a dried rice paddy. There they ordered us to stand in rows, to open our packs and arrange every article we possessed in front of us. Pockets had to be emptied with the inside of each left sticking out so they knew we concealed nothing. Those who were slow to respond were slapped around to convince them that speed was essential. Then each guard examined the items displayed by the prisoner in front of him. I was glad I had so carefully done this in advance.

At one point I heard a guard reacting strongly to some of the items two of our prisoners displayed. Soon he was joined by other guards, all of whom were voicing loud angry remarks. Then suddenly the two men were abruptly yanked to their feet and the guards began beating them with fists, rifle butts, and hobnailed boots. In only moments they were bleeding profusely and covered with bruises. The guards tied their hands tightly behind their backs and roughly shoved them back to the edge of the road. There they were forced to kneel and remain erect on their knees. Then every Japanese soldier or Filipino coming down the road was required to beat them vigorously on their way by. We learned later that at sundown they were beheaded. They had been carrying some Japanese coins among their effects.

The Japanese brought our first day's march to a close about dusk. A few trees grew in the area, but most of us couldn't have cared less. No food was offered to us by the Japanese, but to be honest about it, I only wanted to sleep. Other groups joined us later in the evening but I didn't know they had arrived until morning. It was from them that we picked up the news about the Captain and the Sergeant.

The next morning the composition of our group changed some. As soon as the guards started us forming our columns, some of the men who arrived late yesterday hurried into some of the front positions. I guess they knew how important it was to avoid the end of the column. Since no one owned his position in line it was quite legitimate to move into any spot that was unoccupied. Depending on the health of each individual, positions changed frequently anyway.

Just before orders were given to start marching, a young man about two files ahead of me quickly left his position and ran down the steep bank of the road. As

Japanese soldier beating prisoner if he fell and didn't get up...

he ran he was trying to drop his pants in preparation for a bowel movement. He quickly squatted and put his head on his knees. Instantly a high powered stream of liquid feces came pouring from his body but quickly stopped. He felt great relief from this initial outpouring and started to pull up his pants, but suddenly he was stricken with violent cramps that held him fast. The column was ordered to move out. He began to expel mucous and blood, a sure sign of amoebic dysentery. One of the guards sighted him and was on his way down the bank.

The guard quickly dispatched him with a shot to the back of his head. It sickened me to see it happen, how easily he could have been saved with the proper medicine. Well- equipped aid stations carefully spaced along the route of the march could have saved many lives. Surely in a force of 75,000 men Homma could have anticipated a fair number of sick and wounded. This was an inexcusable oversight on the part of the Japanese if, indeed, it was an oversight and not intentional. By the time the Death March was over I was confident I could resolve that question in my own mind as to what was failure and what was intentional in their quickly formulated plans.

The column continued to move, and the sun bore down on us without mercy. I could tell that despite my week's rest, my body was not used to the demands being made on it during this march. Fatigue was taking over, and I was bone-tired. I hoped I would catch my second wind and pick up my pace again. Oh Dear God, no! Three prisoners just ran from their place in the column and made their way up the bank at the edge of the road. They ran toward the wooded area beyond the rice paddies we were passing at that moment. They must be out of their minds to attempt an escape in broad daylight by running across dried rice paddies where there is absolutely no cover. In a few seconds two guards raced up the embankment and carefully aimed their rifles at the fleeing prisoners. A number of shots rang out and all three men went down. The guards didn't bother to check on their marksmanship; they simply walked back to the road and resumed their march.

When I started on the first day of the march I was rested, moderately well-fed, and sure that I could make it through anything the Nips required of us. As my body began to tire the lack of food, and particularly the absence of water, began to drain my body of energy. At times I began to hallucinate and I could see myself drifting back in the column, then blam, I woke up at the instant the guard emptied his rifle into the back of my head. It took me a moment or two to regain my orientation, to remember where I was at that moment. I knew I had drifted beyond consciousness and I had no way of telling for how long. This really frightened me. I had to be aware of the present or I'd never make it.

There was a bend in the road just ahead of us and we became aware of a group of five very heavy Japanese trucks carrying soldiers toward Corregidor. We tightened our column up and pulled over to the left-hand side of the road as quickly as possible. Lying in the middle of the road just ahead of us were two recently killed prisoners from the column several hundred yards ahead of us. I was surprised that the driver of the first truck didn't seem to know that the two bodies were directly in his path. Then I realized he was well aware of their location and in fact was steering his truck directly toward them. Then I saw his right wheel start to roll over the first body. The tire was very wide and bore a large all-weather tread. In only a moment all five trucks had passed over the bodies and nothing remained except two awkward silhouettes, somewhat reminiscent of the shape of men, flattened completely into the dirt of the road. In a very short time they would be nothing more than two unidentifiable oil spots in the dust.

The heat was taking a heavy toll of our men. To march all day, from sun up to sun down during a tropical summer, was too demanding for many captives. Many had no head coverings and the Japanese would not allow us to get water. There were free-flowing springs at intervals along the Bataan road. They projected the water two to three feet into the air. Yet the Japanese threatened to bayonet anyone who attempted to collect water at those spots. Water was absolutely essential to soldiers marching under the conditions we were forced to observe. The execution of marchers was increasing, drastically.

Today was a particularly wearing day and when the day's march was over I just dropped to the ground and instantly fell asleep. I felt as if I could sleep for a week. I was greatly surprised to be awakened from my sound sleep by one of the guards. I have no idea what the time was. I had a really difficult time trying to get my thoughts together. I was instructed to bring my belongings with me. I fell in line with other prisoners and soon realized we were entering a small metal-roofed shack. At the far end the Japanese had placed a table with several chairs. In each chair, men who looked as if they might be officers sat waiting for the arrival of each prisoner. When I reached one of these men he motioned me to put my belongings on the table. He then picked up my army blanket, unfolded it and examined it for holes or tears. When he assured himself that it was in good condition, he refolded it and put it on a stack behind him. Next he checked my mess kit and likewise found it in good condition. He placed it, too, in a box for metal items also considered good stuff. Finally, he examined my canteen and cup. They apparently met with favor too, so he simply waved the back of his hand toward me indicating that I should go away now. Strictly a one-way transaction. So all my utensils, my blanket, and my canteen were confiscated. All I had left was my musette bag, but with nothing to put in it. I returned to my former resting place and fell asleep immediately.

In the morning, I had nothing to stow in my musette bag so I spent a little time looking over the area where we slept. I luckily found an abandoned coconut half-shell which I scrubbed with gravel. I now had a bowl which I could use as a dish for rice or a cup for water. I quickly put it safely away in my musette bag.

The sun was unusually hot again this day so the executioners at the end of the column were having a field day. I think even the guards were feeling the heat because some of them chose to walk on the other side of the road where a tree-lined area cast some shade. Another big truck came along filled with Japanese soldiers, and I was surprised to see it slowly veering toward our side of the road. I thought the driver might want to keep his load of soldiers closer to the shade. Then I realized they were heading for us, and for no good purpose. I was on the inside row of the column, the one nearest the truck. Then, without warning a soldier leaned way over the truck railing and raked his hand across my face. I thrust my arms up to protect myself, but I was too late. My Air Corps dark glasses had been torn from my face and my helmet was knocked to the ground. There was no way I could rescue my helmet from the ground as it was kicked from place to place, and my dark glasses were gone forever. I felt badly that I hadn't foreseen this maneuver and done something about it. From now on I'd march in the center of the column where no one could reach me.

I lost track of the days and the village names. The only things I could remember were the various incidents that took place along the route. I could depend on the sun; I knew it would be hot. I knew, also, that if I awakened in the morning I was still alive. If we started to march I knew there was at least one day left to go; other than that I was in a mental fog. All I wanted to do was lie down beneath one of those springs we'd seen along the road with my mouth wide open and drink until I could hold no more. Then I wanted to finish off with a clean mattress and a snow-white sheet in the shade of a huge tree where I could sleep long enough to take away the utter exhaustion I felt.

Something seemed wrong: the guards were calling for our evening rest area before dusk. It was a pretty area, by far the nicest we had seen. To the left side of the road, a clump of bamboo was growing much like a giant umbrella and another group of marchers had already occupied some of the space beneath it. When we were dismissed we moved quickly into any vacant space we could find. As I was lying on my stomach arranging my musette bag to serve as a pillow, one of the men next to me spoke.

"Do you see those Jap guards directly across the road from us?"

"Yeah, I see them. Are there about five of them?"

"That's the group. Don't let them think that you're watching them. They've been using us to bury some of those Filipinos over there alive."

"Did you say bury them alive?" I asked with alarm. "That's gotta be the bottom. They can't get any lower than that. I can't think of anything more horrible than burying a man alive."

"Well, if you don't want to be involved, find some way to avoid them when they come across the road. They don't usually pick the same guys twice."

"Thanks so much for the warning. I really don't want that on my conscience."

I figured that must be why they brought us here early; so they could get us to do their dirty work while it was still light. I kept my eye on them while pretending to be busy with something else. At one point they began to stir a bit so I stood up and stretched and actually tried to be ready to move away from them if they started coming my way. It wasn't long before they began to come across the road. I moved slowly but managed to stay on the opposite side of the bamboo from where they made their selections.

When they had picked four men they moved toward the Filipino area. Several of the guards were carrying shovels. The next thing I knew each American POW had hold of either an arm or a leg of the Filipino the guards had selected and was dragging him across the sand and out to a drainage ditch at the rear of the area. They placed the Filipino in the ditch, the guards gave the shovels to the American prisoners, then indicated to them by signs that the Filipino should be covered over with dirt.

Well, as soon as the poor Filipino realized what was happening he became terror-stricken and tried to rise up out of the ditch. Instantly the guards motioned to the Americans to hit the Filipino over the head with their shovels, thus rendering him unconscious. While he lay in that state they managed to complete the burial. I returned to my musette bag and tried to sleep, but I kept thinking about that poor native and whether or not he might still be alive and sufficiently conscious to realize what had happened to him. I had great difficulty getting to sleep.

When we were awakened in the morning I felt tired and sluggish, not a good way to start the day. I tried to keep my mind off the experience I had witnessed last night, but it was impossible. Once again the heat was really intense, sweat poured from our bodies, and the dust caked over the sweat. It seemed we had barely begun the day and already two of our fellow POWs had been killed by the guards. This was not going to be a good day. This was a day to be alert.

By early afternoon everyone of us was really dragging his feet; this again stirred up a lot of dust. I'm sure this didn't help those who were ill. Even the guards were feeling the heat. They became more irritable and mean. They struck many of the men with sticks intending to spur them forward, but the men, too, had very little energy left so nothing of any consequence occurred.

It was already getting dark, but the guards didn't want to stop until we reached a fair- sized city we could see up ahead. I could sense no change in the sun's heat and I imagined that maybe we would have one of our frequent hot nights. By the time we reached the community ahead it was dark and we were as close to being dead as we had been on the whole march thus far. I saw a sign on one of the buildings in town which read San Fernando. This seemed to bring back a memory from the past; this was the end of the march and the beginning of travel by railroad. What a lovely dream, if true.

We heard voices ahead and the clanking of a metal lock as a creaky gate swung open. We pushed through the gate and found ourselves in a fifteen foot high wire enclosure. The surface of the ground was mud—mud everywhere. Mixed in with the mud was excreta of every type and kind, animal droppings and human feces, both liquid and solid. There were a number of bodies littered around the area, people who had arrived before us. They had fallen to the ground and fallen asleep wherever they could stand the stench. We did the same. I was almost sleeping on my feet as it was. All I had to do was relax my knees and I sank to the ground and was gone.

The next morning we arose with the sun. The heat helped to intensify the intolerable odor of our sleeping quarters which, in turn, prompted us to stand erect as soon as possible. We were a mess.

The foul-smelling mud had thoroughly penetrated our clothing during the night. Some pieces on the outside of our clothing were wet enough and heavy enough to roll off and fall back to the ground. Other pieces on the exterior were already dry and firmly attached as if they belonged there until the end of time. When I attempted to move I felt some of the wetter ooze slowly flowing down inside my pants on my bare skin. I could feel the mud on my face getting tight as it dried. As I readied myself to leave I thought of the early lepers who were required to notify all people of their approach by crying "Unclean...unclean." I felt so miserable, I wanted to do the same.

The call for our marching formation rang out, and we happily abandoned our pigsty. Several men had died during the night so they remained in their muddy resting place. Thank God their trial was over.

As we began to form our column many of the villagers stood watching. I had stepped into an outside row but I felt so ashamed to be seen by the Filipino people in my present condition. Among the people stood a young woman with her shy son who was partly hiding behind her, clinging to her skirt. She leaned over occasionally to confer with the youngster. Then he looked up at her questioningly, she nodded yes, and handed him something she had in the pocket of her skirt.

At that moment he left his mother and ran to me. I was terrified! If any guard saw him helping me he would beat him for sure. As for me, there was no telling what the guard might do to me to teach the villagers to stay away from prisoners. Fortunately the guards didn't see him as he slipped a sugar cake in my hand. When he returned to his mother I waited a moment, then when all seemed safe I mouthed the words:

"*Salamat...maraming salamat.*" (Thank you...thank you very much.)

Both he and his mother understood and they smiled radiantly and nodded their heads.

As the column pulled out I began to look forward to the train trip to Capas. How wonderful it would be after our long march to sit in a seat on the train, feeling nice and cool, and watch the landscape roll by.

We really didn't march very far when they brought us to a halt. Guards then walked along the side of the column counting off 100-man groups. One guard was in charge of one hundred men. When the guard escorted our group to the tracks we couldn't believe our eyes. The train consisted of one small-gauge engine and three or four similar gauge boxcars. The doors on the box cars were closed tight, and since they sat in the sun all day they were fiery hot inside. The guard opened the door of our boxcar and ordered everyone to get inside. We tried to get him to wait a few minutes until some of the heat dissipated, but he became very angry and started to use his bayonet to force us in.

We could see he meant business, so the majority of our group quickly entered the door and fairly well filled the car. He prodded, and pushed, and shouted angrily at the men nearest the door. As they began to push, the rest of us had to press harder against the men around us. Finally the guard hung to the top of the door frame, planted his feet on the backs of the last persons in, and pushed with all his strength. When he managed to get all one hundred of us in, he closed and locked the door.

Many men cried out pitifully for air. The heat was so intense we could hardly breathe. The man behind me and the one in front pressed so tightly against me that my feet couldn't touch the floor. I hung in space the whole three hour trip. The boxcar lurched from side to side. One minute I was squashed and gasping for air, the next minute I thought I was going to drop down between the two men who were supporting me and get trampled on the bottom of the boxcar floor.

Men who were sick vomited on the men next to them. Those with dysentery could do nothing to control the frequency of their movements. The foul- smelling gas and liquid excrement they expelled further curtailed the breathing efforts of everyone. I knew even before our trip was over that several men had died. This whole experience was a terrifying one for me.

At the time, I thought I would never survive. When it was all over I couldn't believe I was really still alive.

When the railroad ride from San Fernando to Capas was over, I couldn't remember getting out of the boxcar, or getting in line for the final march to Camp O'Donnell. I think I must have been so numb and so close to death that my mind just shut out the memory completely. I felt like a zombie. I was moving, but I was unaware of how I was moving and where. For some reason, that didn't become clear to me until later, my thoughts reverted to the poor Filipino who was buried alive. I imagined how he must have felt when he suddenly became aware that he was being buried.

In many ways my experience in the boxcar was a duplicate of his, except that I was being buried in bodies rather than in soil. I remember very clearly the moment the doors of the boxcar were shut and locked. The air was fiery hot and there was so little of it. I knew there was not enough air to sustain my life. I knew death was closing in on me. The only way I regained consciousness, now and then, was when the boxcar lurched toward the side which took pressure off my chest and permitted me to draw in a partial breath. So in a real sense I too knew what it was like to be buried alive, but without having to surrender my life.

I couldn't then, and I can't now believe that it was at all necessary for the Japanese soldiers to force us into such terrible conditions just to transport us from one place to another. The ordinary Jap soldier became a wanton killer during the Death March. He killed simply because it felt good to him to kill, and it gave him the chance to use each one of the weapons he carried, in a variety of ways.

Like sharks in the ocean who become stimulated when bait is plentiful and become so excited they enter into a feeding frenzy, the Nip soldier who was stimulated by the great number of ill captives became so excited by the prospect of freely annihilating his helpless, unarmed enemies that he entered into a killing frenzy. Since his officers, who were responsible for his activities, seemed to sanction this killing behavior, thousands of American and Filipino soldiers were murdered during the March.

Perhaps you can understand now why I question the name Death March. To say that thousands of American and Filipino soldiers died during the Death March gives quite a different impression when stated: Kill-crazed Japanese soldiers brutally murdered thousands of American and Filipino captives during the forced march out of Bataan.

Chapter 5

Prisoner of War

We arrived at Camp O'Donnell on April 15, 1942, thinking that once inside the camp things would change for the better and that somehow our diet and medical needs would be met. This was not the case; it would never be the case. All of us entered Camp O'Donnell in terrible physical condition. We had been deprived of food, water, and rest, and had been living under conditions no one would subject the lowest form of animal life to. We suffered from diarrhea, dysentery, malaria; our legs were swollen and our bodies covered with tropical sores. We needed medical attention badly, but it was never given by the Japanese.

The Japanese code of honor dictated that a soldier is honor-bound to fight to the death and that surrender was never an option for the Japanese. Thus, we were not considered as prisoners but slaves to be abused in anyway our masters saw fit. We were told we were their "eternal" enemy and warned that if we tried to escape we would be shot. If we failed to do their bidding we would be beaten. If we failed to salute their lowest-ranking private we would be beaten. If we failed to bow before a Japanese soldier we would be beaten. If we argued we would be beaten. If we requested food, water or medicine we would be beaten. Sometimes the beatings were quick and brief, sometimes they lasted for hours, occasionally they went on for days.

The Japs were great ones for ganging up on a man, pummeling him with their fists until he went down, then stomping and kicking him into unconsciousness with their hobnailed boots.

We did everything we could to avoid raising the ire of our guards, but sometimes just looking in their direction would provoke a senseless assault that so often ended in death.

Of the 7,000 of us who entered O'Donnell, 2,000 Americans died within the first six weeks. We had no medicine, bandages or surgical equipment of any kind, and many of those who died could have been saved had a hospital been set up to receive them. Instead we had a place we called the Zero Ward, where men took themselves or were taken to die. The Zero Ward was a shed in one corner of the compound; it was a place in which no one ever recovered. From the Zero Ward the dead were packed tightly together in common graves in the burial grounds a mile from camp. And they filled those graves at the rate of up to 50 a day.

The huts we lived in were filthy, crawling with lice and other vermin, and acted more as breeding grounds for disease than shelter for us prisoners. The roofs generally leaked, rain blew in through the open sides, and we had no blankets in which to keep warm. Odd as it may sound, pneumonia was a common killer there in the tropics. But then again, in our horribly weakened condition, any disease was a potential killer.

Our diet consisted primarily of a watery rice gruel cooked up in large iron pots. Some days we were existing on 300 calories a day, but in better times we received roughly 600 calories. Basically, we were all starving and anything edible was quickly snatched up and eaten. This included food discarded from the Japs' mess, lizards, the odd snake, some insects, rats and any dogs or cats unfortunate enough to stray into the compound, and sometimes weeds and grass. Anything to keep us going from one day to the next. We were always hungry and were obsessed with food, so much so that at times it was difficult to think of anything else.

We were surrounded by a countryside that produced an abundance of food, but the Japs in their sadistic, mindless cruelty denied us access to that food. And whenever the local Filipinos arrived at the compound gate with gifts of food, they were turned away; some of them beaten in the process.

To make matters worse, there were few water points in the compound and we had to stand in line for hours under the hot sun to get water, which we carried away in coconut shells or the few canteens we were able to get into camp.

Water was always a problem: either there was not enough and we suffered from thirst, or it fell from the sky in buckets, turning the compound into a sea of mud, overflowing the already overflowing latrines and stretching their contents and the disease that came with it throughout the camp.

In order to survive, I had to focus my whole being on survival. I tried to conserve as much energy as I could, vowed I would eat whatever came my way that was edible, and worked hard to avoid the wrath of the guards.

In formations, I tried to position myself within the group so as not to make an easy target for the guards prowling the perimeters of those formations. And, if at all possible, I tried to keep track of the guards' movements without looking their way whenever they were near. Doing so, I was usually able to avoid any direct contact with them, although there were times when nothing I did was good enough to avoid being slapped, hit or kicked. Their punishment was so mindlessly random that it was difficult to avoid.

There was no reasoning to their grounds for punishing us. One Jap in particular, a sergeant named Hashimoto, was extremely violent and unpredictable. He was also an expert at Judo and would demonstrate his ability in the most cowardly manner. We nicknamed him Little Caesar because he had such illusions of grandeur, picturing himself as a great leader of men and an invaluable asset to the Land of the Rising Sun.

Little Caesar would often punch, throw and kick men in the groin, head and face just for the sheer pleasure of doing it. One man he beat so brutally that after that the man was never mentally complete and his speech was impaired. The man's crime had been that he was so violently ill with malaria that he could not work and drew Little Caesar's attention. When a man was beaten like that it deeply effected all of us and we could never understand the cruelty behind it. So, why didn't we rebel and rise up? By the end of the Death March, all of us were so weak and debilitated that we hadn't the strength to fight our captors; our primary fight was to survive. Also, we came from a multitude of units and the chain of command had completely broken down. No one came forth to organize us and lead us.

And shamefully, there were many who would look out for no one but themselves. Fighting often broke out over the scraps thrown to us by the Japs, and there were some who were outright murdered for the food they had, or had it stolen from them and were left to starve.

We were all starving in the camps, but the actions of those Americans who beat and robbed their fellow prisoners disturbed me greatly. That lawless element in camp only served to compound the horrible plight we were in.

Japanese beating prisoner: Little Caesar enjoyed his work

We did talk about escape, dreamed about escape and even made plans to escape. I think escape was on the minds of all of us, but to even attempt an escape brought swift and deadly retribution, and if a man were successful and got away, those in his group left behind would pay the ultimate price!

We were organized into groups of ten and we were responsible for the conduct of each other. At Cabanatuan, I know one man did escape. I assume he got away because we never heard of him again. But the remaining nine members of the group were lined up before a firing squad and shot. Those who were caught trying to escape were tortured for days before being shot or beheaded, so unless a man felt he had a better than average chance of getting away, he didn't take it. Malaria and dysentery were two major health problems in the camp. Quinine was the only drug available to treat malaria, and it was available from the outside, but the Japs refused to allow us access to it. Those who had been able to smuggle money or a ring or watch into camp were able to bribe the guards into bringing in quinine or extra food, but what they brought was never plentiful and the need was always critical.

Malaria was such a terrible disease that it put some into fevers so high that in effect their brains were fried and they became babbling, helpless idiots who had to be helped wherever they went and spoon-fed like infants. Cases like these usually died. Those who suffered from malaria never fully recovered from it and regularly went through bouts of high fever to bone-chilling cold, shaking uncontrollably until the bout, which might last for days, passed.

George graduated from flight training with me and was a member of the 2nd Observation Squadron as I was. We lost track of each other on Bataan, but after the Death March I found him in the prison camp at Cabanatuan. I used to visit him whenever the Japs opened the gates between his section of the camp and mine. We had long talks reminiscing about our experiences while in training and our reconnaissance experiences with the squadron.

Then one day I was on the way to visit him but discovered that the gate between our two sections had been closed off. I was disappointed but planned to try again the next day. Luckily the gate was reopened on the following day and I headed for his quarters. When I arrived the men in his area informed me that he was dead. He had succumbed to some very virulent strain of malaria that took his life within hours. I was shocked. I wandered back to my own building in a daze. I couldn't believe he was gone because he had always seemed so strong and in good health.

Dysentery was a disease many never recovered from. Bowel movements fifty to seventy times a day were not uncommon as liquid excrement streamed uncontrollably from the body. With dysentery, whatever we ate or drank went straight through us, and try as we might to make it to the latrine, we often didn't and had to squat where we were and relieve ourselves. And since the Japs refused to supply us with toilet paper, we had few or no means with which to clean ourselves. Those men who were so weakened by dysentery and could not rise to even make it outside their huts or off the ground on which they lay, were forced to foul themselves over and over, lying in their own filth. Needless to say, the flies surrounded us in clouds and the stench was beyond belief. There were only two types of work to be had at both Camp O'Donnell and Cabanatuan: to carry the dead away and to bury them. In the graveyard, men were packed into holes until they were almost to the surface and then a covering of dirt was heaped on. In the rainy season, with the ground saturated, blood seeped to the surface and it seemed as if the ground itself was bleeding. Also, wild dogs got at the bodies and it was not uncommon to see them gnawing on human bones.

O'Donnell and Cabanatuan were both the same. After two months at O'Donnell many of us were moved to Cabanatuan. It made no difference; each was a dying place. Each was a place to get through one day at a time. We were only existing and days just blended together.

When we did leave O'Donnell, I think even the Japs were glad to see us go because that camp was as close to hell on earth as any place could be.

At Cabanatuan there were 6,000 of us, and at the rate we were dying, I often felt there wouldn't be any of us left by the time the war ended. Every day long lines of men were taken from the hospital out to the burial sites. All of us were terrified of going to the Zero Ward because we knew we would not come out alive.

We did work hard at trying to keep our spirits up, but we had no access to outside news and didn't know how the war was going. What we got from the Japs was all propaganda designed to lower our morale: the Japs were winning everywhere, the American Navy had been sunk, fighting in the Pacific was all going the Jap's way. But most of us knew what they were trying to do to us and understood whatever they had to say could not be trusted.

Still, the much longed-for help did not come and that was a real blow to morale. Each day we waited for some sign that rescue was imminent, but it wasn't until late in the war that we knew for sure the Japs were losing.

I remained at Cabanatuan for four months. Then I was selected, by what means I know not, to go to Mindanao. There we were to join 1,000 men who had been captured in the southern islands at the penal colony at Davao.

Letter to Mrs. Richard Sneddon, July 17, 1942

Norton Gardner Beach, T/Sgt., ~~70~~
Harry Willard Bell, Sgt., Army
Donovan Harvey Brown, Canadian
  Forces
William Michael Delaney, Capt., Army
Michael Francis Dillon, Jr., Navy
John R. Fee, Flight Officer, Army Air
  Corps
Robert Jerome Forbes, Lt., Army
Albert Lewis Gammon, Army Air Corps
William Ellsworth Gray, Army
Earl Bennett Hanson, Capt., Army
Harold Hugh Hirshon, Lt., Marines
Clifford Loren Huntley, Ens., Navy
William Barrere Irvin, Lt., Army Air
  Corps
Donald Ross Macpherson, Ens., Navy
Jerome Rodney Mathews, Lt. (jg), Na-
  val Medical Corps
George Scott Miller, Canadian Forces
Richard Kenneth Murdoch, Lt., Army
  Air Corps
George Edward Nuckols, Army Air
  Corps
Norman Clifton Padgett, Lt., Army
Percy Ellsworth Riker, Jr., Lt., Army Air
  Corps
Murray McIvor Sneddon, Lt., Army Air
  Corps, Killed in action.
Schuyler Killian Van Rensselaer, Army
  Air Corps

HMR/haw/1508

WAR DEPARTMENT

THE ADJUTANT GENERAL'S OFFICE

WASHINGTON

AG 201 Sneddon, Murray M.
(7-7-42) OG.

July 17, 1942.

Mrs. Richard Sneddon,
  11215 100th Avenue,
    Edmonton, Alberta,
      Canada.

Dear Mrs. Sneddon:

    I have your recent letter concerning your son, Second Lieutenant Murray
M. Sneddon, O-407072, Air Corps, who, according to the latest information
available, was serving in the Philippine Islands at the time of the final
surrender.

    Lieutenant Sneddon's name has not appeared on any casualty list re-
ceived in the War Department. It is reasonable to assume that in the last
days before the surrender of Bataan there were casualties which were not
reported to the War Department. Conceivably the same is true of the surrender of Corregidor and possibly of other islands of the Philippines.
The Japanese Government has indicated its intention of conforming to the
terms of the Geneva Convention with respect to the interchange of information regarding prisoners of war. At some future date this Government
will receive through Geneva a list of persons who have been taken prisoners of war. Until that time the War Department cannot give you
positive information.

    The War Department will consider the persons serving in the Philippine
Islands as "missing in action" from the date of the surrender of Corregidor,
May 7, 1942, until definite information to the contrary is received. It is
to be hoped that the Japanese Government will communicate a list of prisoners
of war at an early date. At that time you will be notified by this office in
the event his name is contained in the list of prisoners of war. In the case
of persons known to have been present in the Philippines and who are not reported to be prisoners of war by the Japanese Government, the War Department
will continue to carry them as "missing in action," in the absence of information to the contrary, until twelve months have expired. At the expiration
of twelve months and in the absence of other information the War Department
is authorized to make a final determination.

    (CONTINUED NEXT PAGE)

    This notice of my death was printed in a magazine published by U.C.L.A.
When my parents received it they were terribly shocked. Of course they
immediately contacted the War Department starting a correspondence that
lasted for a year or two. Obviously the report was untrue, but the seed of
doubt had been sown. They were never really able to cast that doubt aside
until I met them face to face.

Negotiations are being made through the Department of State and the International Red Cross, to secure permission for the safe conduct of foodstuffs and other articles for prisoners in the Philippines, also to have an accredited representative there to attend to matters relating to prisoners. The Japanese have not granted the desired permission up to this time, but it is hoped that the negotiations being made will result favorably.

For information regarding communication with prisoners of war you should contact your local chapter of the American Red Cross, who will assist you in every way possible.

A memorandum regarding benefits to certain dependents of missing, captured or interned personnel is inclosed.

Very truly yours,

J. A. ULIO
Major General,
The Adjutant General.

1 Incl.

Chapter 6

To Mindanao and the Davao Penal Colony

Near the end of 1942 many of us were moved by ship to the prison at Dapecol. The penal colony had been a maximum security prison for hardened criminals who, prior to our arrival, had been moved to a leper colony on the island of Palowan.

Our camp was basically a huge farm of many thousands of acres. On it were grown coffee, avocados, coconuts, a variety of vegetables, rice, and bananas. However, almost all of the food was exported by the Japanese, and in spite of living in the midst of a wealth of agricultural abundance, we were to receive very little of it. Our diet was made up mainly of rice, an occasional vegetable, and whatever snakes, rodents and insects we could catch and eat. We never rose above a starvation level of sustenance, and all of us were never more than walking skeletons.

Still, the Japs worked us for long and brutal hours in the fields, never taking into account our diseased and weakened conditions. Basically, we took each day at a time and concentrated everything we had on getting through that day. Those who could not or would not bring themselves to make the effort to get through each day were soon dead.

The camp itself was laid out in neat, orderly rows with huts lined up much like those in a military camp. At each corner of the prison compound there was a guard tower. Surrounding the compound was a triple fencing of barbed wire, and the guards had orders to shoot anyone who approached the wire.

We had roll call, or tenko, twice a day: once just after sunrise, then again just after sunset.

The guards themselves were a very unpredictable, bitter group of men and we never knew what might set them off, as they would become violent over anything and everything. All of us worked hard not to draw their attention and subsequent wrath, but even that didn't work. Just being in the immediate vicinity of a guard could, and often did, bring on a beating for no cause whatsoever. All of us lived in fear of them, but at the same time could not help but make fun of them whenever we thought we could get away with it.

Behind the barracks were three latrines, each latrine having 20 holes to accommodate our needs. They were rank, infested with flies and every insect imaginable, and were generally very unpleasant places in which to relieve one's self.

We slept on beds made of boards with no covering. There were no mosquito nets to keep off the periodic clouds of flying bloodsuckers, and we were living in one of the most malaria-infested areas of the Philippines. Malaria was a disease we all suffered from and no one seemed to escape.

Our work week was seven days long with two days off each month, and all day long it was "speedo"—hurry up—from the Japs. Everything we did had to be "speedo," but we didn't have much to give as there was no "speedo" left in any of us.

I worked in the rice fields where we spent long days in deep mud, bent double at the waist, planting rice shoots in the goo we toiled in. We planted in neat rows along a rope that was stretched across a diked field. Each time we finished a row, the men holding the heavy, wet rope had to put everything they had into moving it and keeping it stretched tight for the next row.

Failure to keep up with the planting, failure to keep the rope taut, failure to stay on your feet despite illnesses brought on beatings that went from a few slaps to the use of rifle butts. The Japs were so into beatings that they even lined us up facing each other and made us take turns slapping the man opposite. They were sick, sadistic, brutal little bastards who knew no end to the violence they took pleasure in dishing out.

Days ran together in camps like O'Donnell and Davao. I prayed a lot, asking God to watch over us and free us from this place by bringing the war to a swift and triumphant end. The Japs had to be beaten; they couldn't go on as they were and dominate the world. I somehow knew God would not let that happen, but wished He would hurry it up, get it over with, and get us home.

As the days ran together, I often lost track of them. Only a significant event—the death of a friend, a beating, an extra bit of food—stood out in my mind as being something different enough to hang on to, whether it be hope or bitterness.

For the most part we merely existed.

Then one day, for a reason never entirely clear to me, I was transferred to the camp at Lasang.

HJW

WAR DEPARTMENT
THE ADJUTANT GENERAL'S OFFICE
WASHINGTON

AG 201 Sneddon, Murray M.
(12-24-42) PC-G 360052

January 6, 1943.

Mrs. Richard Sneddon,
11215 100th Avenue,
Edmonton, Alberta,
Canada.

Dear Mrs. Sneddon:

Report has been received that your son, Second Lieutenant

Murray M. Sneddon, O-407072, Air Corps,

is now a prisoner of war of the Japanese Government in the Philippine

Islands. This will confirm my telegram of December 28, 1942.

The Provost Marshal General, Prisoner of War Information

Bureau, Washington, D.C., will furnish you the address to which mail may

be sent. Any future correspondence in connection with his status as a

prisoner of war should be addressed to that office.

Very truly yours,

J. A. ULIO
Major General,
The Adjutant General

1 Inclosure. Memorandum re Financial Benefits.

Prisoners planting rice

Prisoners resting at filthy barracks in the prison compound

Interior barracks: lice and bed bugs were prevalent

Chapter 7

South to Mindanao

Official Report

Partially reprinted from the Bureau of Naval Personnel Information Bulletin, March 1994 issue. From the Ex-POW Bulletin, Volume 54, October 1997, No. 10.

The Japanese took 1,000 men left Cabanatuan on October 26, 1942. The men were crowded into the hold of a 7,000 ton British-built freighter at Manila for shipment to Davao on the island of Mindanao, with stops at Cebu and Iloilo.

The voyage took 11 days. The hold was filthy and vermin-infested. Some prisoners were lucky enough to get a place on the junk-filled, rain-swept deck. Two men died on the trip. On 7 November 1942, the Americans were unloaded at Lasang Lumber Co., near Davao Penal Colony. The sun treatment for two hours followed, and then the group were forced to march more than 15 miles to the penal colony. Many were so weakened they fell by the roadside. In this instance, Japanese picked them up, threw them into trucks, and carried them along.

It developed that the Japanese commanding officer at the penal colony, which in peace times had been operated for criminals by the Philippine Bureau of Prisons, was disturbed when he saw the condition of the Americans. He had requested able-bodied laborers. Instead, he shouted, he had been sent walking corpses.

In spite of the condition of the prisoners, they were without exception put to hard labor. No clothes were issued until American and British Red Cross supplies began to arrive at Davao described as "the salvation of the American prisoners of war."

Food was slightly better at Davao. In addition to rice, the prisoners received once a day a small portion of mango beans and some *camotes*, green papayas, cassavas, or cooking bananas. However, most of the prisoners already were suffering from beri-beri and the food was not sufficient to prevent the disease from progressing. Although oranges and lemons were abundant in the vicinity, the Japanese would not allow prisoners to have them. The brutality of Japanese officers continued. One Lieutenant habitually beat prisoners. This Lieutenant had done most of his fighting at the rear when in action, and had been assigned to prison duty as punishment. He avenged himself on the prisoners.

The camp commandant made a speech to the prisoners shortly after their arrival. "You have been used to a soft, easy life since your capture," he said. "All will be different here. You will learn about hard labor. Every prisoner will continue to work until he is actually hospitalized. Punishment for malingering will be severe." These orders were rigidly enforced.

The arrival of two Red Cross boxes for each prisoner early in 1943 caused joy beyond description among the prisoners, according to the statements of three officers. The boxes contained chocolate bars, cheese, tinned meats and sardines, cigarettes, a portion each of tea, cocoa, salt, pepper, and sugar. Most important of all, quinine and sulfa drugs were included. The Red Cross supplies had been received aboard a diplomatic ship in Japan in June, 1942. The prisoners never learned why it took them seven months to reach Davao.

Prisoners greeting the arrival of Red Cross packages

In April 1943, one of the American prisoners, a hospital orderly, was wantonly murdered by a Japanese sentry. The orderly was digging *camotes*, outside the hospital stockade and directly beneath a watch tower. It was an extremely hot day. He called to a fellow prisoner to toss him a canteen from the stockade. As the orderly was about to drink from the canteen, the Japanese sentry in the tower shouted at him angrily. To show that the canteen contained only water, the orderly took it from his mouth and poured a little on the ground. Apparently because he did this, the sentry trained his rifle on him and fired. The bullet entered at the neck and shoulder and came out at the hip. The orderly cried out: "Don't shoot me again." The sentry fired two more bullets into the man's body. He then emptied his clip at the man inside the hospital stockade, who ran for his life and was not hit.

Chapter 8

Lasang— My Fourth, and Final, Prison Camp

On March 2, 1944, just one month short of our second year as prisoners, the Japanese sent 650 of us from the main camp in Davao to a new camp on the outskirts of the village of Lasang. This new camp lay some twelve miles south of Davao. Our departure left the main camp with approximately 1,250 men. Our group was officially designated as a "work detail." The Japanese commander of prisoners insisted that we be the 650 healthiest men in the camp. Most of us had been slogging around in the mud and muck of the rice paddies for the past year or more. The Nips promised that we would find our new prison camp much improved over the old one, and that we would receive better food and more of it in our new location. The promise of more food alone seemed to make the move worthwhile. To go through each day, year in and year out, with agonizing hunger pangs gnawing at our bellies made life seem hardly worth living.

As our truck convoy pulled up to the prison gate we saw promise number one vanish into thin air. In no way could we rate this camp physically superior to the camp we had just left. This camp was small—unusually small—and tightly ringed in by the barbed wire fence. At some points the wire was only ten to twelve feet from the building. Since our guards prohibited us from going near the wire on threat of death, it was obvious that our freedom would become even more restricted than before.

When I first walked through the main gate at Lasang, I had in mind finding a space where I could enjoy some quiet part of the time. It seemed to me that a corner would be ideal. I'd have a man on one side of me and a wall on the other.

I rushed past the first three buildings and entered the last one. Perhaps in this way I'd have a little time to pick my spot.

Prisoners working in rice paddies: poles cut into shoulders.

Filipino laborers built these barracks, I was certain. Although they appeared to be bare bones as far as refinements were concerned, they were well-made. There were no nails; everything was bound together with long thin strips of rattan. Large diameter bamboo poles formed the primary structural skeleton of each building. Nipa palm branches covered the gable roof and woven rattan formed the outside walls. The building sat directly on the ground. The builders framed openings that functioned as windows, but they remained openings—no glass. The same was true for doors. There were six total: one at each end, two in each side. They too were simply openings. Flat, woven panels slightly larger than the window openings were hinged at the top, and held open at the bottom by a stick. This permitted a small measure of control over wind or rain, but since the door openings had no covers weather became an inside problem as well as an outside one.

Rain water flowed freely over the ground beneath each building and in a short time all aisles could turn into a slippery sea of mud. When rain or wind were not a factor and all openings were unblocked, insects entered readily. The mosquitos in particular were a hazard. Malaria was one of our most common ailments.

The arrangement of aisles divided the building into six equal bays. In each bay a solid platform of wood planks, approximately fourteen inches above the ground, completely filled in the area between aisles. These sleeping platforms did manage to keep us above the ground, but the hard surface of the boards raised havoc with our bodies. We had lost so much weight that protruding hip bones, shoulder blades, and shoulder joints soon became locations for bed sores and bruises for many prisoners.

When I entered the building I walked quickly down the central aisle until I reached the rear exit. Just inside the exit I turned left, put down my small field bag—which I used as a pillow—and loosened my bed roll. A double layer of thin canvas beneath my army blanket afforded me some insulation and kept the blanket clean.

My bedding took up a space two feet in width. At the head of the bed my field bag held the remainder of my worldly possessions, a military issue mess kit and the most prized of all my belongings, a relatively new toothbrush.

On the Death March the Japanese confiscated all my field gear, but due to the great number of deaths in our first prison camp, Camp O'Donnell, I was able to get another blanket and mess kit. I spent my first two months at Davao Penal Colony in the isolation ward of the prison hospital suffering from amoebic dysentery. There a medical corpsman gave me a toothbrush for Christmas. I couldn't hold back my gratitude. I cried openly, and through the sobbing tried to express my thanks. It was the most appreciated Christmas gift I have ever received.

Prior to that time I used to visit the camp kitchen where we prepared our food. I picked up a few pieces of charcoal and mashed them into a fine powder. By wetting my forefinger with a little saliva I could get the powder to stick. Then, by using my finger as a toothbrush I tried to clean my teeth. The gift of a real toothbrush made it easy to do the cleaning and made me feel like the wealthiest and cleanest man on earth.

Not long after I had completed the arrangement of my belongings and thereby laid claim to this last space in the bay, a fellow prisoner who looked to be about my age stopped and looked at the space next to mine. He hesitated for a moment then spoke.

"Are you saving the space next to you for someone in particular?"

"No," I answered. "It's yours if you want it."

He promptly spread out his gear and began to organize some of his things against the wall at the head of his bed. I figured from the amount and type of articles he was pulling out of his bag he was probably captured on Mindanao. When he pulled out a large section of mosquito netting I knew for sure I was right. He also pulled out one or two extra pieces of clothing that were neatly folded— worth a king's ransom in my opinion.

Those of us who made the Death March out of Bataan entered prison camp with nothing more than our "dog tags" and half a coconut shell in which to put any food we might be fortunate enough to receive. I envied him; that was the honest truth. But Mindanao was hot and humid. If I devoted a moment of serious thought to the matter, I could recognize clearly that clothing ranked very low on our list of needs.

Most of us wore nothing more than a Japanese G-string. The garment consisted of a cloth tie sewn across the top of an eight by thirty inch panel of cotton. The wearer tied the tie around his waist with the cloth panel hanging to the rear. Then he bent over and pulled the panel to the front, tucked the panel end under the tie and allowed the remaining cloth to hang down in front. Except for the fact that it was made of light cotton, it closely resembled the early breechcloth worn by the males of many Indian tribes. For the Jap soldier it was an undergarment; for us it was our entire wardrobe.

Satisfied with the appearance of his new home, my new neighbor turned toward me, extended his hand with a smile and said, "By the way, my name is Jon. That's J-O-N, without an H."

"Pleased to know you, Jon. I'm Murray."

He was a pleasant-looking guy, clean-cut, very fair skin. I couldn't help but wonder how he tolerated the sun with such a light complexion. He had a quick smile, a set of teeth that would have warmed the heart of any dentist, and an upbeat attitude that was worth more than gold to men who lived in a wearying state of depression as we did.

Judging on the basis of our first meeting I liked him, but I had grown very wary. I wasn't sure just how far I wanted anyone to enter into the inner sanctum of my life. I had suffered the loss of so many close friends over the past two years, losses that left me devastated and near the brink of giving up. I was certain I couldn't handle many more.

If I had known that within a few months I would lose Jon, too, I might have cooked up some lame excuse, gathered up my few belongings, and moved to another space in the barracks. I didn't want to experience another loss of someone I truly cared for. I left Jon at this point and went out the rear exit of the barrack to check the facilities outside.

The Japanese located latrines between two of the four buildings, and they placed wells for bathing not more than 15 feet from the latrines. The wells were eight-foot-wide holes dug into the earth and ending below the water table. The water was muddy and would remain so indefinitely. A wood platform about ten feet square overlapped one edge of each well and on both platforms a single five-gallon bucket with a rope attached awaited the first bather.

It didn't require a genius to see that as a bather hauled up buckets of muddy well water and poured them over his sweaty, work-begrimed body, the contaminated water would have to run down the sloping platform and cascade back into the well. As time went on we knew we could expect further contamination of the water by the seepage from the nearby latrine, too.

Most of all, we were aware of the chaos that would result when 650 men arrived at the compound gate after the day's work with only two buckets available for bathing. No soap was in evidence anywhere. We had been prisoners for years and had never received a single bar of soap in all that time.

The compound area was bare, no source of shade anywhere. Our location lay only six degrees above the equator; the days were invariably scorching hot and muggy. Without hats—those were not issued either—many would suffer from overexposure to the sun. The kitchen was a small replica of the one we had left, but it remained to be seen if the food would be an improvement.

The following morning we got up early and headed to the kitchen for break-fast. We were served a small portion of boiled rice, nothing more. So much for dreams two and three; they also vanished. Our food did not change with respect to quantity or quality.

After cleaning up our mess gear, we headed for the front gate and lined up in a column of fours inside the compound. The gate was opened wide and the col-umn slowly moved out. Armed guards counted each line of four men and reported the totals to the senior "non-coms." Just beyond the perimeter of the cleared area outside the camp, a narrow graveled road climbed slowly up the brush-covered rise ahead of us.

The Japanese had denied us permission to wear shoes since the beginning of our imprisonment. Our feet had toughened some but not enough to withstand the knife-like edges of the layer of rocks which covered our narrow road. It proved excruciatingly painful to traverse that mile or so path twice each day for the six months we worked in that area. Many of us finished the walk with bleeding feet.

As we neared the end of the graveled road the view opened rather abruptly. Ahead of us lay a wide clearing resembling a section of highway under construc-tion. The center section had been graded, surfaced with coral, and rolled flat. On both sides of the clearing a dense jungle of tall trees defined the width of the cleared area.

In the distance the trees extended across the end of the clearing, marking the end of development in that direction. On the left side, in front of the trees, stood a few randomly placed huts; near them extended a neat row of Japanese fighter aircraft. It was obvious to us that we were standing on the runway of a burgeon-ing military airfield.

We were furious! For God's sake, didn't they know that to use prisoners to work on projects or arms that would be used against their own countrymen was a flagrant violation of the rules of land warfare? Had they never heard of the Geneva Convention? We protested. They utterly ignored our protest. They informed us that the Japanese government had not agreed to the Geneva Accords. If we didn't work we would receive no food—end of conversation!

They immediately put us to work clearing and leveling the area adjacent to the runway, then packing it with coral. To assure our complete cooperation we were surrounded by Japanese soldiers armed with rifles and fixed bayonets. Anyone who wished to carry the protest further would have to do so on his own, but he would run the risk of being killed instantly. We had seen that happen before.

As soon as we returned to the prison compound we discussed our predicament at length. All were in agreement: to hold out for a principle at the cost of our lives was a poor trade. Only one approach seemed possible, and it would have to be followed with great caution. We would do the work we were assigned, but we would do it at the slowest pace that was safe. Oh, we would appear to be working busily; we just wouldn't accomplish much.

We knew the Japs bitterly hated us. They welcomed any provocation that gave them a reason to kill us. So we decided to tread a path somewhere between the amount of work they wanted from us and the amount of work we felt they might accept. It was a dangerous game, but one we were willing to play. We hoped we could make adjustments before any loss of life occurred.

For the first two or three days our stalling tactics did not provoke any major incidents, but we knew the Japs weren't happy with our progress. Then one ten-man group failed to convince the soldiers that they were really trying to complete their work and the guards reacted angrily. They forced all ten men to kneel in a row with their hands tied behind their backs. A few guards entered a nearby brush-covered area and returned with a handful of dead limbs. They carefully placed a trimmed branch behind the knees of one man and extended it across to the same position on the next man.

When all ten were similarly prepared, they pushed each man back so he was forced to sit on his feet with the branch tightly locked between his legs. Each one was forced to sit very erect with his weight well back—it was impossible to ease the pressure exerted by the weight of the upper torso. Any man who tried to shift his weight forward had a rifle with fixed bayonet thrust toward his chest.

Each guard delighted in seeing how quickly he could make the thrust and how close the point of his bayonet came to piercing the body of the prisoner. Each prisoner held his position. It was obvious from the clenched teeth and furrowed brows that they were feeling extreme pain, yet they dared not move. In a short time they lost all feeling in their lower legs, yet the guards were in no mood to call a halt to their game.

I felt my stomach muscles tightening, my breathing rate increasing, and anger coursing through every part of my body, but there was nothing I could do. Any action on my part would have resulted in a severe beating or death. I could only look away, work harder, and try to bleed off the anger I was feeling. After more than 30 minutes the men were still maintaining their position.

In the distance I could see some of the Japanese "non-coms" forming a column of prisoners to begin the march back to our prison compound. Soon the guards in our section began to do the same. We gathered our tools together in one area and began to form a column. Just before we were ready to move out a couple of the guards untied the hands of the ten, then started yelling. They pointed toward the column and made threatening thrusts with their bayonets to get the men to move quickly into the formation. The prisoners freed themselves easily from the branches but when they tried to rise to a standing position they teetered wildly, stumbled and fell down.

To balance while erect on legs devoid of feeling was more than they could handle, especially while being threatened by the guards. After several disastrous attempts, they clung desperately to each other and staggered crazily into the column. The rest of us immediately adjusted our positions to accommodate the ten so they might continue to support each other. The column began to move. Each of the afflicted ten tottered forward with feet held wide apart, hoping thereby to avoid a fall.

As the circulation began to return to their legs the pain was unbearably intense. Their heads lolled forward, then back. Their eyes were locked tight, faces were pinched into deep furrows radiating from the point where eyes and brows met, and over and over each man prayed in a harsh whisper, "God, help me! Oh, Dear God, give me strength to make it through the gate!"

They were beginning to learn, as each of us from Bataan had learned full well from the Death March, that to grow weary of the struggle, to fail to maintain position in the column or to fall behind the column, marks a man for death, and there is no waiting period. This type of punishment was so characteristic of the Japs. They treated a prisoner in such a way that he lost the ability to maintain his balance, then killed him because he fell down and couldn't keep up with the column. They beat a man into unconsciousness with a club, then when he fell to the ground they bayoneted or shot him to death because he failed to follow the order to stand at attention. Well, in this instance it didn't work.

The ten tortured men very quickly recognized the trap they had been led into, and through sheer terror of the imminent death they faced summoned all the energy they could muster and stumbled through the main gate. Had the distance to our prison camp been longer, they all might not have made it. Luck was on our side this time.

I often felt frightened for Jon's safety. One day when we returned from work on the airfield he came down the main aisle of our barrack cackling to himself and said, "That crazy Nip out there thinks I'm a cowboy. He called me a vaquero."

I knew that what he had been called was *bakkeru*, which usually carries the meaning, "fool." He had obviously done something which had angered one of the guards. The fact that he had been singled out by the guard was a potentially dangerous situation. I felt it was always best to remain a faceless being among many, to refrain from doing anything that might draw attention to yourself. Jon seemed unconcerned about the incident, so I didn't make an issue of it.

Jon's confrontation with the guards reached a high point late one afternoon as we were returning from the airfield. We had been working a little farther away from the rest of the prisoner group, so it took us more time to return our tools and enter the formation. Jon and I wound up in the very last row. He was on the outside right of the column end. I was next, at his left, and there were two more POWs to my left.

It had been a tiring day. The heat from the white coral surface of the runway rose like shimmering tongues of colorless flame and distorted the image of the near distance as if it were a desert mirage. We felt half-sick from the long exposure without head covering of any sort. As a result, men walked with their heads bowed, each lost in his own thoughts. No one spoke. We just concentrated on getting one foot ahead of the other.

When we reached the end of the airfield and started down the rock-covered road, Jon became very uncomfortable. Like many other prisoners, he had very tender feet. His twice- daily trek over this sharp surface always upset him, but today, coupled with the heat, I suppose he felt almost as if the Nips had planned that rock-filled hazard just to annoy him. He was walking with that peculiar gait that many of us adopt when we are trying not to let our full weight reach our feet. Apparently the two young guards walking behind us thought his efforts quite comical because one of them reached out with his toe and kicked Jon's raised rear foot into his weight bearing leg, causing him to stumble momentarily. It was a malicious prank used by school boys the world over, but quite thoughtless in this case.

What happened then I will never forget. Jon instantly jumped straight up, whirled his body around 180 degrees to face the guard, came down in a crouch with his hands raised to shoulder level and contorted like claws, his mouth turned down, teeth bared and let out a loud "Y-A-A-A-H." The guards both blanched white, nearly fell over backwards, and almost dropped their rifles. He gave them a real scare.

At that point Jon straightened up, threw his head back, and laughed heartily. Turning again to march with the column he wagged his head from side to side as if in disbelief at the childish behavior of the young guards. Then he resumed the low cackling laugh I had heard from him before. He must have been enjoying the memory of the guards as they almost fell over each other in fright. The soldiers initiated the whole episode; there was no doubt in my mind about that. The fault was theirs, but Jon's reaction was dangerous.

We continued to march down the road toward the compound and it seemed to me that Jon was no longer walking with the mincing step he had used before. He strode proudly forward with head held high, shoulders back, and a big smile on his face. He was satisfied that at least the guards knew they couldn't try any of that kid stuff on him. The incident was soon forgotten and we resumed our plodding march to the prison compound.

When we arrived at the gate, we had to stand and wait for a bit. The front of the column normally had to check its alignment so that each file of four men could be counted in. This usually required a little adjustment in ranks, however there seemed to be some other holdup because the column wasn't moving at all. We began to look toward the front gate to find out what was causing the delay.

Lieutenant Hoshide, the camp commandant, was there on his white horse looking down upon everything around him. His officers, non-coms and soldiers were gathered around him. The conversation switched rapidly from one to another then suddenly stopped. Those of his retinue who were in front of him swung back out of the way and several pointed in the direction of our end of the column.

I began to feel very uneasy when a group of non-coms started heading our way at a brisk walk. They looked very determined. It seemed to me they were pointing and looking straight at me. I almost stopped breathing for a moment and my stomach began to lock up with fear. I quickly tried to review my day. Did I, without realizing it, do something that directed their anger toward me? Because of my sudden panic, I couldn't come up with a single idea before they roughly battered their way into the formation, scattering prisoners like tenpins.

I tensed my body waiting for the first blows to land, but instead they brusquely knocked me aside, surrounded Jon, and made off with him. Then I realized that the two soldiers whose prank started the trouble were bringing charges against Jon. Obviously, they wouldn't mention their part in the affair.

The soldiers who grabbed Jon pushed and jabbed him ahead of them on their way back to the spot where Lt. Hoshide and the higher-ranking non-coms were waiting. He half-ran most of the way. He had no choice. They struck him from every side and shoved him in the general direction they wanted him to go. The rapid battering from all sides confused him completely. In a short time he had no idea which way he was moving or what was really happening to him.

He was turning backward at times, then lunging forward. Many times he almost fell to the ground. When he finally stood before Lt. Hoshide he was teetering back and forth trying to keep his balance. In a moment we saw a soldier step toward Jon and the next thing we knew, Jon was hurled to the ground and lay flat on his back. Instantly every soldier in the group ran at Jon, kicking him viciously with their hobnailed boots. Some began to stomp on his stomach and chest. Jon instinctively rolled over, pulled his knees tightly up to his chest, lifted his arms up to protect the sides of his head, clasped his hands across the top of his head, and put his forehead down on his knees to protect his face. The savage kicking continued for some time, then at a command I was unable to hear, the guards withdrew and left Jon lying half-conscious in the dust. During this entire episode I think I felt every blow and kick that Jon received. I was weak and fully washed out when it was over. I could imagine how Jon must be feeling and I was afraid that now they might finish him off with a bayonet thrust to the chest or a bullet through his skull. Fortunately, however, Lt. Hoshide, who fancied himself quite a leader of men, decided to use this event as an object lesson for us.

Ignoring Jon's need for attention, he proceeded to lecture us on the dire consequences of threatening any Japanese soldier. His words were translated for us by "Running" Wada, the camp interpreter. His command of English was extremely elementary and very difficult to understand. Not much information reached us in a form we could understand.

Eventually several prisoners were permitted to carry Jon to his place in the barracks, and the rest of us were counted in. The bruises and lacerations he received pretty well covered his entire body. Our doctors examined him carefully and recommended that he be confined to his bed for at least three weeks. At first he was hardly able to move without feeling extreme pain, but slowly he began to improve. Not having to work on the airfield was an important factor in his recovery. Jon was fortunate this time. He escaped death, but in less than four weeks his luck was destined to run out.

Japanese beating prisoner, often kicking with heavy boots

August 17, 1944 dawned clear and hot. There was certainly nothing particularly distinctive in that beginning, at least not in the southern Philippines and at this time of the year. To prisoners of war, all days and nights seem but carbon copies of each other. There was no reason to believe that this day or this night would be any different from the hundreds that had passed.

But during a war, time generates a different rhythm. Long periods of quiet create great apprehension and stress, because every soldier knows that at any moment violence and death may erupt without warning.

The war had left us two and one-half years ago when all American forces in the Philippines were surrendered to the Japanese. From that day to this one, we concerned ourselves solely with survival. We had no knowledge of the war. We couldn't be sure that our forces would ever return to set us free.

To endure in the face of such bleak prospects required much more than simple faith that it would happen. Too many men saw no reason to keep going. They couldn't deal with a life which offered no promise of improvement in its future. They died by the thousands. They died within days of entering our first prison camp.

Those of us who endured those past two and one-half years did so, I believe, because we were forced to come to grips with the essential needs for survival in a hostile world. First of all, and I think the most important of all, we tried to survive only this present day. We ignored the future because we had no access to events that might enable us to make plausible predictions about its outcome. We also learned to give no merit to any rumor, no matter how much we might hope for its consummation. We simply blocked it from our minds instantly. And finally, we learned to attach no significance to the war news fed to us by our Jap guards.

They, of course, delighted in telling us their forces were winning every major battle, and that our country was heading for sure defeat. We couldn't survive in the face of this kind of verbal barrage if we accepted any of it as truth. We would die from severe depression in less than a week. So all malignant reports of that type were instantly denied access to our thoughts.

We muddled through our work at the airfield this day without incident despite our usual effort to appear very busy without really getting anything done. We traversed the road to the compound in good time and the guards ushered us through the gate with all accounted for. We showered, ate supper, and retired to the barracks for rest and recreation.

A few men, when captured years ago, managed to bring a deck of cards into camp and enjoyed an ongoing round of bridge or poker. Most of us simply spent the evening in conversation with friends, or lay back and watched the gecko lizards on the ceiling spear unwary moths with their long tongues.

About 9:30 the call for "lights out" drifted through the barracks and soon darkness ended all activity. The only light visible was the occasional weak ray that entered the door openings from the lights on the guard towers outside. Most of us crawled back on our sleeping platforms and bedded down for the night. A few voices continued for a while but soon they too trailed off and faded away. Silence settled over the camp.

My desire for sleep was pushing me toward limbo when a faint droning sound lured me back again toward consciousness. It was very difficult to hear at first, but for some reason my mind felt challenged to identify it. It could be an insect somewhere just over our heads roaming back and forth from one side of the bay to the other, or it could be a larger object way off in the black, distant miles beyond our camp.

Once it disappeared completely, but soon emerged again sounding a little bit louder. I was certain the noise was increasing in volume and I began to feel more and more sure that it sounded very much like a distant airplane, and not just any airplane. I was willing to bet money that it was indeed an American airplane.

I was fully alert now. My heart was beating quite a bit above normal. I was trembling in anticipation. I began to question all my past experience as a pilot to back up my judgment. I knew Japanese engines had individual exhaust ports jutting from each cylinder; this gave the plane a rapid popping sound somewhat similar to a motorcycle.

American planes, on the other hand, had collector rings around the engine which received exhaust from each cylinder and fed the expended fuel out a single exhaust port. The resultant sound was a constant and continuous drone, just like the plane that was circling over our heads this very moment.

I know every man in the barrack was awake, despite the fact that not a sound could be heard from any of them. Their attention was riveted to the sound above us, and although all of us felt sure in our minds that we were listening to an American plane, our past experience was at work cautioning us against another disappointment.

In reality we had only a few moments to wait for the proof we hoped for. Our ears were suddenly attracted to a new sound—the rushing sound of heavy objects plunging down through the night air—and then sharp staccato explosions as bombs slammed into the airfield that we had been working on only a few hours ago. This was the proof we had been waiting for. After an eternity of two and one-half years we now knew: Our forces were returning to take us home!

Thank God! Thank God! Thank God! At last our most fervent prayer was being answered: life was taking on a new dimension. My eyes brimmed with tears of joy, and my thoughts flashed homeward. Maybe our long-hoped-for day of freedom was closer than we dared think. In prior years we dared not allow ourselves hope for the future, because we were always dealing with rumors from unknown sources. Now this bombing by our forces, in our presence, inflamed us all with new hope.

Our newly resurrected hopes were quickly cooled, however, when we heard shouts from the guards outside. We could hear the heavy beat of their footsteps as they ran toward the gate to the compound. Then the outside lights were all turned off and the entire camp was plunged into darkness.

Soon we realized that the entire guard company had entered the compound and formed a ring around each barrack. A guard stood at each opening of the building with rifle and bayonet thrust forward, ready to quell any attempt by prisoners to take aggressive action. Hoarse whispers from leaders inside the barrack warned prisoners to stay on their sleeping platforms and to remain still.

The incident had reached its peak and was now waning. The plane had droned off into the distance. We prisoners were making every effort to remain calm, and as a result the guards were slowly relaxing their vigil. A night's rest could help us to see things more clearly. It was time to sleep. I was in such a highly agitated state, however, that my mind refused to settle down. Questions kept intruding into my thoughts.

Would we be treated better or worse now? If the Jap officers had been leading their troops to believe that Japan was winning the war, how would this American attack change their outlook? Would they become more fearful? Would our guards tend to act more irrationally as a result?

If our forces should invade Mindanao, would our captors abandon us and look to their own survival, or would they kill us all before leaving? Would they take us all with them to Japan to serve as hostages in defense of their homeland? Answers to these questions were vital to all of us, but my first assessment left me fearful and anxious.

After years in their custody, I understood how fanatically the Japanese pursued their aims and how ruthless they could be in eradicating anything, or anybody, that stood in their way. We were their enemies and we were in their possession; they could use us in any way they pleased. They weren't about to let go of us for any reason. They would kill us first!

The night passed without any further disturbances and we awoke early in the morning. Because we were anxious to see the damage at the airfield, we ate quickly and headed for the compound gate. After forming our usual column of fours, we waited for the order to leave for work. Eventually "Running" Wada, the interpreter, arrived and made an announcement complete without the letter "l," which is not used in the Japanese alphabet, and for which he substituted the letter "r."

"Arr American sordjers wirr have hariday—wirr not go to work."

We were really disappointed we would not see the results of the bombing, but were happy to receive a holiday.

The first night after the bombing I again had difficulty getting to sleep. My thoughts drifted toward my family again. I wanted so much to get home. I could see the image of my parents before my eyes. My mother tended to be the family worrier. I'm certain she shed many tears and offered countless prayers on my behalf. I was really concerned that my years as a prisoner might have an adverse affect on her health. If I managed to survive and to return home, I greatly wanted to be sure that she would be there too. After what I had been through already, I couldn't bear to learn of a loss in my immediate family when I returned home, especially if it were one of my parents.

Our family was a close one. Although my father was at work most of the day, he always found time to help me with my homework in the evening. He arranged lessons for me with the highly regarded professional of the Los Angeles Tennis Club so I could improve my game. He even volunteered to play tennis with me on Saturday mornings.

He was certainly everything a young boy could hope for in a father. He was both a chemist and a professional writer. I admired him so much for his abilities. He was even a very accomplished amateur magician and card manipulator. He kept the neighborhood children mystified with his clever tricks. He, too, was constantly in my thoughts.

I couldn't wait to see my little sister, Delta. When I left for the Philippines she was a chubby, freckle-faced kid. By the time I might get home she would be a young lady. If she turned out to resemble her mom she would also be called an "attractive" young lady. I was six years older than she, so at times she impressed me pretty much as a pest. But I knew that I would see her quite differently when I returned, and I looked forward to having a cute sister as a companion.

The girl of my dreams, Fiona, whom everybody called Fee, had been in my thoughts often. When I was assigned to the Philippines I thought of marrying her and taking her with me. What a beginning it could have been for us to travel such a great distance, to a very exotic place. Our lives could be filled with wonderful adventures and during vacations we could travel to Hong Kong, Bali, Java,

Singapore and other equally exciting places that most people never see in a life-time. But my conscience talked me out of such a choice.

I was an inexperienced, newly trained military pilot. If I were fatally injured in an accident, my young wife would become a young widow thousands of miles from her friends and family. I felt that was a risk I didn't want to take. Now, as a prisoner of war, I felt vindicated in my choice. War was not in the picture when I first reached my decision. Now I think of how terrible it could have been if she were imprisoned in a civilian prison camp in Manila and I were interned in a military camp several hundreds of miles away. I'm sure the guilt I would feel for placing her in such jeopardy would have finished me off.

I was convinced that I wanted Fee to be my wife. She exemplified everything fine and good in a woman. Not only was she a beautiful girl outwardly, she had all the special qualities that made her beautiful within. She was a caring person, sincere, loving, devoted to her family, always wanting to be helpful to others. There was no doubt in my mind that she was a real treasure. Yet, here I was thousands of miles away from her, rotting in this God-forsaken concentration camp, and with no chance to tell her how very much I loved her and how desperately I wanted her to wait for me.

The odds of my getting home were, at best, astronomical. The odds of her waiting for me for years were, at least, staggering. Putting the two together, I figured my chances at about a million to one. These flights of reasoning obviously didn't do much to elevate my desire to do my best to keep struggling on, so I drifted back to reality committed to do my best to stay with today's problems only. With that mental adventure concluded, I soon fell fast asleep.

The scenario for the second day after the bombing turned out to be precisely like the first—another holiday. I began to feel uneasy. It was not like the Japanese to keep us idle like this. Something was about to change. Perhaps something radically different was in the offing. I tried to stay on the alert. I didn't care for surprises. The Nips were conspicuous by their absence. They must be preparing for something, but what?

If we had known in advance what was about to happen in the next twenty days, I'm not sure it could have made any difference in the outcome. When events of staggering proportions are suddenly thrust in our way, reasoning alone can't possibly determine who will survive and who will not. Such an event was about to overtake us. Its nature would be so cataclysmic that almost 90% of our POW group would be violently and cruelly killed!

Chapter 9

Journey
to Oblivion

When our forces bombed the airfield where we had been working, we were really elated. We reacted with great joy and enthusiasm. We visualized ourselves in American hands within a couple of months; however our main interest at the moment was to learn what the Nips intended to do now. Two days had passed since the bombing and as the morning sun awoke us on this the third day, we wondered if the Japanese might give us some hint of their plans.

We could understand their spending a couple of days or so, to smooth over the damage on the airfield before sending us back to work. Usually, if we were unable to perform one job for any reason, the Nips assigned us to another. Once, instead of working at the airfield, we dug ditches around the outside of our compound to divert the flow of rain away from our living quarters. We had never before been kept idle for more than a day.

Our present routine of one vacation day after another worried us because it was out of character for the Japanese. We soon began to feel fearful again; our joy and enthusiasm were waning fast. The longer the delay, the further our imaginations ranged. Some men now considered a wholesale execution of all POWs a real possibility. This kept all of us on a constant alert.

Our usual careless banter ceased. The faces of many prisoners became grim, and their eyes revealed the fear they felt inside. They searched suspiciously for any unusual Japanese activity beyond the barbed wire. Everyone hunted for even the remotest of clues that might warn of impending action against us. We looked for any increase in the number of guards in the towers, or patrolling the barbed wire between the towers. We checked to see if any of the perimeter guards carried new weapons. We searched for any evidence of stockpiling, either of weapons or ammunition, in the guard towers. We even kept track of Lt. Hoshide and his senior non-coms to see if they checked the perimeter guard company more often than usual. All these observations seemed important to us.

The Japs had already had ample time to reach a decision on what they planned to do. As work time grew near we again lined up at the gate inside the compound awaiting word to leave for the airfield. The gate remained locked. There were fewer guards outside the gate than usual. The few who were present stood at ease, with rifle butts on the ground, hands overlapped and resting on the top of the barrel. Bayonets were sheathed. Their relaxed position and lack of readiness did not suggest they were awaiting any activity soon. Then, in the distance, we saw "Running" Wada scurrying toward us as fast as his bent body would permit. He entered the compound somewhat out of breath from his effort; took a few deep breaths and delivered his announcement.

"Arr American sordjers wirr go to barracks and get berongings. You wirr reave dis camp."

With that said he hurried out the gate and disappeared in the direction from which he had come. For a brief moment all of us stood motionless. We had been awaiting a decision, and there it was, but we were somewhat surprised by the radical change in the Japanese position. After sending us to Lasang for a job we assumed was of paramount importance in their minds, they were now, six months later, withdrawing us from the project and heading elsewhere.

Perhaps the Nips were suddenly frightened to learn that our forces were so close at hand. They must surely realize now it was only a matter of time until our troops would move in on them. Maybe they were ready to abandon their holdings in the Southern Philippines and high-tail it for home. We quickly broke ranks and with heads now filled with new questions, hurried back to our individual barracks to pack our belongings.

As I began to roll up my blanket and the protective canvas beneath it I asked Jon what he thought might happen to us now.

"Who knows. These crazy Nips are apt to do most anything. I can't see them sending us back to Davao Penal Colony. According to rumor, the guys there were all evacuated two months ago."

"Do you think we can really believe that rumor?" I asked as I put my blanket roll under the straps of my musette bag and cinched them down tight.

"Hell, yes. It came from a good source. Do you remember those two very sick guys in Barrack Two?"

"You mean the two who had dysentery so badly?"

"Yeah, that's the ones. They sent a beat-up truck from the main camp with two Jap guards and one POW corpsman to help take them back to Dapecol. Well, the corpsman let the word out that they were going to be evacuated soon. His guess was they would be sent back up to Manila."

"Do you think that's what will happen to us?"

"Hell, I wouldn't be the least bit surprised. After all, if our troops are returning wouldn't it make sense for these sadistic bastards to move us north toward Japan? They're not going to let go of us. They're going to get every advantage they can muster from us. The only way we'll ever be free from them is if we escape, or if our armed forces finally defeat them. It's as simple as that!"

I confess his analysis made good sense, but in all honesty, much of the time good sense failed when applied to the Japanese. I was ready and anxious to return to the main gate. I didn't want to be caught idly passing the day in conversation with Jon when the Nips were in a hurry to leave. I asked Jon if he were packed and ready to go, but he said, "I still have some things to decide on. Why don't you go ahead and I'll join you as soon as I can." I quickly left the building and got a bit of a surprise when I saw how much activity was taking place outside. As prisoners walked up to the forming columns-of-four, we were brusquely pushed into place by the guards. All outside men, that is those who were on the edge of the formation, were tied to each other with ropes that threaded through several belt loops of their pants, or were tied to their wrists if they were wearing a G-string. The rope passed from one man to the next all the way along one side of the column, across the rear to the opposite side, then forward to the front of the column and across to the beginning. This tactic convinced me that the Nips knew now that all the fairy tales they had been feeding us about their many victories lay naked and exposed. The bombing of the airfield had laid bare that lie. It was very obvious they now feared us much more than they'd led us to believe.

We outnumbered them by a five-to-one margin but they still possessed the weapons. At some moment in the future when we were in a massed group and they were gathered around us, we might just be able to change that balance without losing too many men. However, it now looked like they had considered that possibility because here we were bound into a formation which made it impossible for us to carry out any such plan. When the Japs finished encircling all elements of the formation with ropes so no man could escape, the gate was opened wide and we left Lasang for the last time.

I wasn't really happy about leaving. I didn't trust the Nips. They were always devious about their intentions. I was suspicious of their every move, and because their decisions involved us, I was really fearful of what might lay in store for us. We had no idea where we were going or how we would be treated on the way. If I had a choice of gambling with my future, or staying in a situation which wasn't good but where I knew the risks, I would choose the latter.

As the column moved out a few yards from the gate, the Nips suddenly directed the lead element to swing sharply to the right. The prisoners on the outside edge of the column immediately felt a great strain exerted by the ropes. The men forward of their position tugged hard in order to travel the extra distance required to make the turn; the men behind them, who had not yet reached the turning point, became a dead weight pulling in the opposite direction. Meanwhile, the prisoners on the opposite side of the column were over running the men ahead of them. To ease their own pain, the prisoners on the outside of the column, those most affected, began to yell. "Dammit, you guys in the rear. We're getting pulled apart up here! Get your butts up here, fast!"

The noise attracted the guards, who approached the problem in their usual way by thrusting their bayonets at every prisoner on the outside of the turning segment of the line. This, of course, provided no help and moved the situation closer to chaos than it had been in the first place. The threatened men pulled with all their strength to move the men behind them faster toward the front of the formation. Only in this way could they avoid the thrusting bayonets. However, the ropes prevented any increase in forward speed for only the outside line of the column. It was obvious that the only solution lay in having the other marchers walk more slowly. Eventually, by slowing the whole process down, we managed to negotiate the turn and get everyone headed in the new direction. The prisoners at the head of the column, where the problem first occurred, were relieved but some were nursing sore wrists rubbed raw by painful rope burns.

In front of us lay a dusty dirt road bordered rather closely by dense shrubs about twelve feet high. All vegetation on both sides of the road had been reduced to tones of gray and brown. It was likely that during a period of considerable rain the plants had shot up to their present height, then were seared by the sun and drained of all life when a period of drought followed. Viewed through the dust raised by our shuffling feet, they took on the appearance of a ghostly "highway of death." I wondered if this was a premonition of something ahead and I shuddered momentarily as the thought ran through my mind. Then I chided myself for allowing such fantasies to grow unhindered in my normally guarded thoughts. After all, the physical appearance of all the elements in the landscape were quite normal; I just needed to keep a tighter rein on my imagination.

The sun was once again bearing down on us without mercy. We were sweating heavily. The rising dust found ample moisture to cling to since our wet bodies were barely covered with clothing. But the sun was not our only problem. The Japanese insistence that we march in such a tightly bound formation caused us to walk abnormally and had us treading on each others heels constantly. Our energy and patience were just about at an end. Something needed to change, and fortunately something did.

It was a slow change, but it was enough for us to sense, and therefore gave us relief from the tension we were feeling. The foliage at the roadside retreated a good deal and slowly began to come down in height so we could get some feeling for where we were going. Then suddenly we could see glimpses of water ahead. We had arrived at a dock on Davao Gulf.

There in front of us lay a Japanese freighter with her gangway already in place for embarking passengers. On the dock, bales of unknown products bound with huge strands of manila hemp sat waiting to be delivered. Immediately the guards began to untie our fetters and yell out "*Yasume*" (rest). I quickly sat down in the shade of one of the larger bales, laid my head back and closed my eyes. The relaxation felt heavenly.

I had hoped that I might have a chance to find Jon, but I was sure he must be quite a bit behind me and I was too tired to use up my rest time searching for him. I was sure the Nips would not permit me to wander aimlessly around anyway. I later overheard a couple of men estimating that our walk must surely have been about two or two and a half miles long. Under the restrictions placed on us it felt to me like it was at least three times that length. It was obvious we were destined to board the freighter and probably sail for Manila, but I was too tired to deal with it now. I tried hard to block the voices out of my mind and in no time I fell fast asleep.

I have no idea how long I slept, but I awakened when I heard the sound of lively conversations and friendly ribbing going on all around me.

"Hey, Mike. I see you still know how to *yasume*."

"Hell, yes. But what about you guys? We marched all the way here from camp, and you drive up in a truck like the idle rich."

"Live and learn, live and learn."

It surprised me to see that the Japs had just brought a new contingent of men to join us. The enthusiasm stemmed from the fact that these men made up the 100-man work detail that left our main camp a short time before we did. So we were happily greeting old friends whom we thought had already been evacuated north. Our excitement bought us no time from the Nips, however. Our full complement of 750 men had now been reached and they wanted to get us on board immediately. So before anyone could exchange much in the way of news, they herded us all together and led us in a single line to the foot of the gangway.

This was not the first time I had sailed on a Japanese prison ship, but I had very poor memories of the last occasion. As our line reached the deck the guards grasped the shoulders of the first man and shoved him to the left, the second they pushed to the right, and so on. Many men who had come up the gangway together with a friend were startled by being suddenly separated. When they tried to change directions and rejoin their friend they were intercepted and angrily bashed with a rifle butt or shoved back to their assigned route. If Jon had been behind me or I behind him we would have suffered the same fate.

It was my lot to be sent left to the forward cargo hold of the ship. A long wooden ladder had been lowered into the hold and the top couple of rungs projected above the rim of the open hatchway. Each of us stepped up to the ladder, turned 180 degrees around, and then cautiously made our way down the ladder to the floor of the hold below. The floor was bare: normally it would have been filled with cargo. The bales we rested against on the dock probably came from this hold. I quickly chose a spot against one of the walls so I could rest my back against something firm. As I looked back up to the sky, the open hatch seemed a long way from where I sat.

When all 375 men had wedged their way into the sea of bodies on the floor of the hold, the guards removed the ladder. Then we truly experienced the dangerous situation in which we had been placed. We were packed into that hold like the fish in a tin of sardines. Every man was resting against at least two other men. Those in the center had it even worse. They depended on the men around them to just sit in an upright position. In every sense of the word, we were trapped with no way to get out.

The ship was made of metal which retained the sun's heat and radiated it to all parts of our compartment. When we entered the hold we left all moving air behind; we were living in a sweat box which had never been designed for humans. When I first took my position against the wall, I could feel a mild vibration on my back. From that I surmised that the ships engines were warming up in preparation for our departure. Now it was evident from the movement of the clouds in the sky above that we had left the dock and were slowly under way south to the mouth of Davao Gulf.

The ship's movement was quite slow, yet the heat in the hold was cooling a slight amount. I could detect no fresh air entering the hold, but it was possible that the air passing directly over the hatchway might be causing a siphoning affect, drawing the stagnant air we were re-breathing up and out of the hold. The smell of sweating bodies and road dust was already being assimilated into the lingering aromas of former cargos, and now a new element was about to be added.

Suddenly the faces of two of our guards were peering down on us. They began to lower, on ropes, a group of five-gallon gasoline cans. The tops of the cans had been trimmed off and hoop-shaped bails were attached. This enabled the cans to serve as buckets. Each bucket was removed from the hook and the rope was retrieved for the next one. In all, they must have lowered 15 or more before the two guards disappeared. At first we thought they might be lowering food to us. That was too much to hope for; all the buckets were empty. Then it dawned on us. These containers were meant to hold our human waste.

It was clear to us now. Not only would we have to live in a hot, steamy, crowded space, but we would have to endure the equivalent of open-pit latrines in the very heart of our living quarters. The cans had to be positioned on the spot to which they were lowered because they would be withdrawn from there when full. So now there was an angry adjustment for every prisoner in the hold in order to provide room for the men whose spaces were displaced by the buckets. Our spirits hit rock bottom when we realized we were going to be confined in this miserable atmosphere for the entire voyage. In effect, we were living in a giant bathroom with no air conditioning, and with toilets that couldn't flush.

Shortly beyond mid-morning I sensed a sudden but almost imperceptible change in the movement of our ship. Wondering if anyone else had noticed it, I turned my head to the right and spoke to the prisoner who was jammed against me on that side.

"Did you just notice a change in the way our ship was moving?"

"Yeah," he said. "Did you notice it too? It seemed almost like we rode up over a bump in the water. What do you think caused it?"

"I'm really not sure, but I wondered if it might be because we're getting close to the place where Davao Gulf meets the open ocean. So far we've moved steadily forward without feeling any rolling or side movement. I remember when I first left the States to come to the Philippines our ship sailed up San Francisco Bay very smoothly. Then, when we moved out into the ocean, we began to roll strongly from side to side as our ship was lifted by swells which moved across the ocean one after the other. Maybe this is the first hint of an ocean swell.

Maybe it means we're about to leave the Gulf and move out into the open sea. That's my guess."

"You could be right. If you are, we should know soon. We should feel more just like that first one, but maybe bigger." With that said, he lapsed into silence as if giving the matter more thought. I turned my head forward again.

After a moment or two of silence between us I realized I had not told him my name, nor had I inquired about his. So, turning my head toward him again I said "My name is Murray, by the way. What's yours?"

"Mine's Liz," he replied.

"Liz! How did you ever get that name?" I thought of saying that it sounded like a girl's name, but I decided not to get off to a bad start with a guy who was going to be jammed against me for the next couple of weeks or so.

"Well, it's really a nickname given to me by the guys in my barrack at Davao. When I was at Davao Penal Colony I worked everyday at Mactan, planting and harvesting rice. By any chance did you work there, too?"

"Yeah, I was there. Every day, just like you."

"Then you probably know what it was like at harvest time."

"In what way?"

"Well, I remember the first days of harvest when all the water had been drained out of the paddies and the mud became cracked and hard as concrete. The stalks that had been real green turned a yellow color and the heads of rice were so heavy they bent over at the top."

"Yeah, I remember that, too. As a matter of fact it's about the only nice memory I'll take with me if I ever get home."

"When work started, we moved into the dried paddies dragging those big baskets behind us to put the rice in. Then we grabbed as many stalks as we could hold, cut them off below our hand with that curved, saw-like knife and dropped them in the basket. Then, a lotta times, when we got closer to the middle of the paddies, we heard a loud scurrying sound ahead and everybody stopped, because we knew it was."

"A monitor lizard!" I said, finishing his sentence for him.

"Right! Well, I guess you know what happened then. A group of us surrounded him and started to creep toward the spot where we thought he was hiding. Then, when he figured we were close enough, he put on a burst of speed, ran right between two of our guys, and dove over the dike into the next paddy. Well, I wanted to catch one of those speed merchants in the worst way. I knew it would make a good meal for me and a lot of my friends, if the Nips would let me take it back to the compound; but we had to catch one first. Y'know, some of those things grow to be as much as four feet long!"

"Liz, those things are vicious; their teeth can really rip you apart. Did you ever get your hands on one?" I asked.

"Never did. They're too fast. Once they get over the dikes and into the next paddy they're safe. The guards won't let us go after them. But I never lost the hope of getting one. It almost became an obsession for me. I spent so much time thinking of a way to bring off such a capture that the guys in my barrack started calling me 'Lizard Man.' Then it got shortened simply to 'Lizard,' and finally just 'Liz.' I guess I deserved it; I just couldn't stop thinking about the damn things. You know how it is when all you can think about are ways of getting some food."

"Yeah, I sure do. Did you ever try to…" My words were suddenly cut off in mid-sentence by yelling from the Japanese up on the deck above us.

Although I couldn't understand a word they were saying, it seemed to me those voices were shouting in fear. Almost instantly we heard anti-aircraft guns firing from our ship. POM…POM…POM…POM. Once again I felt the tense knots of anxiety gripping my stomach. We were back in the war again, but this time we were even more helpless than before. We were happy at Lasang when we knew our planes were able to reach our area. Now, in this floating coffin, we didn't want our planes to come anywhere near us. Our ship was unmarked. Our forces had no way of knowing we were aboard. We were at their mercy. All we could do was sit and wait to be hit! The firing didn't last long, but it was intense for a time. Then, as suddenly as it started, it stopped.

What a relief to draw a breath again. I think from the time the firing first started until the episode was finished, I stopped breathing. The knots in my stomach struggled to untangle and the tenseness in my arms caused me to tremble all over. I could see that if other instances such as this one continued to take place, it could become a long, nerve-wracking trip that might sap the life out of us long before we reached Manila. I turned to Liz and asked "Are you okay? How are you feeling, Liz?"

He hesitated for a moment, then replied in a quiet voice I could barely hear, "Like warmed-over death. I don't need any more of that in my life. I feel so helpless crowded in here the way we are with no foxholes to protect us, nothing to hide behind, no place to run. It's one thing to fight against your enemy with weapons you have been trained to use, but it's something else when you're waiting to be fired on by your own forces and you can't move an inch in any direction.

Y'know, these Japanese bastards are so stupid. All they would have to do is paint the large letters 'POW' on the deck and on both sides of this old tub and they could sail from here to Japan and no one would fire on them. But no, they've got to do it the hard way. So maybe they'll get ripped apart in the water by our planes and we'll all get killed with them."

I understood his rage and his fear as his thoughts moved back and forth between the anger he felt at being used by the Japs and the depression he plunged into when he felt helpless to do anything about it. I put my head on my knees and began to pray silently.

By early afternoon our ship made contact with the mountainous swells of the open sea and rolled vigorously from side to side. This relentless motion soon intensified the feelings of discomfort brought on by half-buried elbows, hips and knees which had been denied movement for too long. Through sheer necessity, and by common consent, we began to shift positions, lifting, leaning, turning slightly in one direction or another, stretching legs and arms until every one in our area had achieved a new degree of physical comfort.

Inasmuch as no new attacks had threatened our safety in the past couple of hours, we also attained a moderate degree of mental comfort as well. Once again I let my head roll back until it touched the bulkhead behind me. I closed my eyes and began to doze off. The next thing I knew, Liz was nudging me in the side.

"Hey, Murray—look! The Nips are passing down more cans."

"Maybe this is what we've been waiting for," I mused. "They've gotta feed us some time."

"Well, I'd question that last statement, but let's see if you're right."

We watched the prisoners unhook the cans from the ropes, then thread their way carefully and ever so slowly through the mass of bodies before them, doling out measured quantities of rice and what appeared to be water. When our turn finally arrived each of us received one small scoop of rice and four ounces of a thin soup made from potato peelings. Two servings this size made up our daily ration for the trip—barely enough to sustain life, for a while, that is. After our Jap guards withdrew the empty food cans we saw no more of them for the rest of the day.

Fading light in the hold warned us that night was coming soon. Total darkness would soon settle over us and movement across the hold would become hazardous at best. Many prisoners decided to make the trip to the latrine area right away while there was still light enough to pick out a safe route.

Men suffering from dysentery had no choice: as soon as the first hint of bowel cramps started they moved rapidly toward the assembled buckets. Due to the crowded conditions in the hold, there was no chance they could make the trek to the buckets in time. When they could no longer control the violent cramps they were fighting, their stomachs erupted in an explosion of foul-smelling gas and liquid excrement that splattered on themselves and on the men over whom they were stepping. The polluted prisoners struck out blindly, flailing their arms and cursing the men who had contaminated their bodies and clothing with such filth.

The offending prisoners could do little more than whimper an apology and return back to their place in the hold. With tears streaming down their cheeks they suffered the ugly rebukes of those they had offended. Without medicine there was no way they could bring under control the ravages of the disease that put them through such humiliating experiences. Also, they knew they were doomed to repeat these degrading performances many times during the night with similar consequences.

On the morning of the second day the rolling motion of the ship caused the sun's early rays to rake back and forth from one side of the hold to the other. I awakened when a blinding flash of light fell momentarily on my upturned face. For a time I felt somewhat disoriented; then I remembered where I was and what day of our trip lay ahead. I tried to move, but my body seemed paralyzed. I was locked in so tightly by my fellow prisoners that I had been unable to move during the night. The lack of circulation temporarily rendered me immobile. An extended period of brisk massage returned the blood flow to my limbs and body, but at the cost of intense pain.

After providing for my immediate comfort, I became aware of a marked change in the quality of our atmosphere. I turned to Liz and said, "Liz, are you awake?"

"Yeah, sort of. What's up?"

"Have you noticed how awful the smell is in here? It's really foul!"

"Yeah, I know, and I know why. I made a trip to the john as soon as it became light, and the mess over there by the buckets is unbelievable. The cans overflowed during the night and the stench is really terrible. None of the poor guys in that location could move so the stuff just flowed in on them. God, they must feel miserable. Y'know, between the guys with dysentery and the overflowing cans, we're soon going to be living in a latrine, not around one."

Even though the ship continued to forge ahead, the air quality failed to improve, due probably to the stink rising constantly from the urine and excrement in the brimming buckets and on the floor of the hold. As the morning sun heated up the interior of our living space, the heavy smell of sweating bodies arose to join the existing stench and render it more rank than before. The added humidity seemed to increase the weight of the air and made it very difficult to breathe. God, how could anyone be expected to live day after day in such filth? We didn't have enough water to drink, so how could we spare any to clean our bodies and the space we occupied? We couldn't live like this, at least not for long. We'd die of depression, if nothing else. Of course, this is what it always boiled down to: the Nips didn't have the least concern for our lives. Why did we think it should be any different? We'd better recognize that in their minds our lives would have absolutely no value. If we thought differently, we'd just have to develop a new patience that did not consider comfort a valid factor.

Nothing occurred to change our problem until midmorning. At that time a guard peered over the edge of the hatchway for a moment, then quickly withdrew. In a few moments he was back, and joined by a second guard. Both studied the floor of the hold below for several moments, then thrust the end of a long wooden ladder over the edge of the hatchway. A few prisoners below the base of the ladder stood up and guided the feet into open spaces between limbs and bodies below. At that point one of the guards stretched out his arm and displayed two fingers on his closed hand, a signal that the prisoners below took to mean that he wanted two men to come up the ladder. Two men who had helped to guide the ladder into place instantly scrambled up the rungs to the top and stepped over onto the deck.

We lost sight of both men for a time, but soon they were visible at the edge of the hatchway, lowering one of the ropes with a metal hook attached. It was then that we understood that the two men would be removing the latrine buckets and emptying them over the side of the ship. One of the men cupped his hands to each side of his mouth and called down to the prisoners in the vicinity of the dangling rope, asking them to place the hook under the bale of the nearest bucket. This was quickly accomplished and the men drew the line taut, ready to begin the withdrawal process.

The events that followed, for some strange reason, were not anticipated by any of us. As the men above lifted the first bucket off the floor, the rope and its attached weight became a giant pendulum. Immediately the rocking motion of the ship took charge and swung the bucket way out across the center of the hold. As the heavy can reached the peak of its arc a large portion of its contents poured over the side and rained down on the men below. Instantly angry yells arose from all men in the hold, "Pull! Pull, dammit. Get that thing outa here!"

Unfortunately the two men on the deck had their hands full just to hang on to the increased weight of the swinging bucket. To their credit, both men reacted quickly. One of them dropped to the deck in a seated position, braced his feet against the outside of the hatchway, and held the rope tightly. This placed the burden for bearing the weight on the lip of the retaining wall around the hatch rather than on his own arms and shoulders. The second prisoner leaned well over the edge of the hatchway and grabbed the rope as far down its length as he could. By exerting all his strength he was able to pull the bucket up a few feet and the man on deck took up the slack and prevented the can from sliding down again.

This procedure was working well until the oscillating bucket struck a glancing blow against a pipe that supported the underside of the deck. Instantly the can began to spin wildly and as it whirled around more of the contents were flung onto the apprehensive prisoners below. As time passed, the two workers on deck became more sensitive to the problems they encountered and on occasion were able to hoist their heavy loads up to the deck with relatively little spilling.

When the job was finished, the men on deck returned down the ladder, fully expecting a chewing out from the men below. However, many of us realized they had a nasty job and had probably done as well as anyone could under similar circumstances. As soon as the men returned to the hold, the two guards withdrew the ladder and set it aside for later use. The prisoners who had been struck by the splattering debris were really upset, and they muttered angrily as they continued to try to clean up their gear and clothing. The two men who emptied the buckets gained a measure of respect when they gave us an account of their time on deck.

"When we carried each bucket to the side of the ship to empty it, we were surprised to see that the Japanese were steering a course just two or three miles off shore. By following the contour of the shore line they probably figure there is less chance of being discovered, and if attacked they can quickly run the ship aground. For us, and especially those who are able to swim, we can more easily reach shore if the ship is disabled." This was indeed good news and our spirits rose to a new high.

An hour or so following the bucket-raising episode the Japs lowered the first of our two meals for the day. The menu was unchanged from yesterday's meal; the same inadequate quantity remained unchanged. Our late afternoon meal contained no surprises either, and once again the Nips quietly disappeared until the next morning. Before night closed in, we again made a last trip to the "honey buckets," as we spitefully called them, and it was evident they were close to overflowing even then. After darkness settled over us I didn't feel completely ready for sleep, so I ventured a last remark to Liz.

"Liz."

"Yeah?"

"Y' know, the stink of this hold is so bad that the Japs can't even stand to come up to the edge of the hatchway."

"I think you're right, but boy, how I'd like to yank a few of those slant-eyed bastards in here for a few days to see how well they'd make it living like this. And wouldn't it be great to arrange with the guys topside to spill a whole honey bucket full of real choice shit right on top of their heads!"

I could tell even without being able to see him that he had a dreamy look of pure joy in his eyes and a sadistic smile a yard wide on his angelic face. I couldn't resist the chance to say "Now who's dreaming, Liz? You're a real sadist, you know!"

"Yeah, damned right. I can't tell you how satisfying it is to think of the Nips enduring the same treatment they force on us."

Without hesitation I said, "I understand perfectly. We're all doing it. Anger wells up in me often, and I yearn to be face-to-face with any one of our guards, without weapons, just bare hands. I think I could tear him to shreds in a few minutes, my anger is so intense. They should pay with their lives for the inhumane treatment they heap on helpless prisoners."

I sat lost in thought, mulling over what I had just said. I was surprised to hear the words of killing someone slide so easily from my lips. I had been a faithful church-going youth and thought I had always advocated turning the other cheek and forgiving my enemies for their trespasses against me.

But now this was not an impersonal judgment I was making. I was the object of the mistreatment and I found myself filled with hatred and ready and willing to take the life of another. To make matters worse, I viewed my thoughts as both normal and justifiably right! I think this was the first time in my life that I was wholly in touch with my deepest feelings and not relying on someone else's tenets or rules for answers. I felt pretty well depleted after the wrestling match with my conscience. I didn't want to talk further so I just quietly said, "'Night, Liz."

"Night, Murray. See ya in the morning," he replied.

Day Two ended.

Day Three of our voyage began much like the first two. When it was time for our volunteers to go topside to empty the honey buckets, they worked much faster to pull the cans up and thereby reduce the effect of the ship's motion. Although they failed to avoid spillage altogether, they did curtail it considerably. When they returned below decks again they reassured us that the ship's crew was still directing our course along the contour of the island. This mode of travel obviously increased the time of our voyage by a considerable amount, but because we had a better chance for survival we were willing to endure it.

Our midmorning ration of food was delivered without ceremony. Still no change in quality or quantity. Because of our inability to clean up the conditions contributing to the build-up of odors in the hold, however, the air became heavy and dank as well as foul-smelling. To eat our food in this atmosphere became more and more difficult. Yet for our own welfare we dared not pass any meal by. Some sensitive prisoners couldn't keep their food down and the sour stench of their vomit added to the build-up in the hold.

In the early afternoon the sudden sounds of loud voices on deck drew us once again to a full alert. Almost instantly a machine gun began firing long inter-mittent bursts. Soon a second machine gun joined the first and the voices increased in pitch. Was it just a drill, or was it for the purpose of fending off an impending attack? My God, how could we be sure? We couldn't understand a word they were saying. Many men sat stiffly, shielding their eyes against the sun with one arm and anxiously searching that portion of the sky visible to them from their position in the hold. They searched for planes but fervently hoped they would be unable to see any.

As I scanned the gaunt and frozen faces in front of me, I could see the fear and anxiety emanating from the eyes of every man. Our bodies, held rigidly in suspension, seemed paralyzed by the din above. My mouth was bone dry. I was clutching my legs to my chest trying to make my body as small a target as possible. I let my head bow down to my knees and silently cried out in despair "No, Dear God—no! Don't let it happen now when we have no way to protect ourselves."

Yet I knew as I uttered the words that I had made a foolish prayer. What did I expect? Did I expect God to stop bullets in flight? It seemed to me that among the many gifts God had given us, one of the most precious was the gift of intelligence. He bestowed it on no other creatures, only mankind. In my mind I could imagine him saying, "I gave you intelligence so you could see the wisdom of sitting down with other groups of my children and discussing your needs. If you act alone, what you do may infringe upon the rights of others without your being aware of it. If both of you work together, first on one group's problems then on the other's, and continue this way until you find some promising solutions you will, with intelligent compromises, be able to bring about an appropriate course of action for each of you.

"Because you worked it out together, you will develop respect for each other and love will grow between you. How much better this is than holding only to your own view and never considering the legitimate needs of your neighbor. Since you demand that only your solution be considered, your differences grow out of proportion. The patience of each of you grows thin, the use of force seems to be the only way out.

"Once war starts there is no way back. Then, sadly, the innocent suffer the same fate as the guilty. When the war is won, not because the loser's cause was wrong, but usually because he lacked the resources of the winner. It often requires centuries to eliminate the ill will that has grown between you. Often the loser seethes with hatred and vows someday to wreak vengeance no matter how long he must wait. So ill will is perpetuated, many young soldiers and innocent civilians die, but nothing is changed. Only hatred remains.

"I grieve for you with all my heart because of the terrible way you are being treated. However, I cannot arbitrarily change the laws of the universe, which I carefully designed for all my children, just so I can perform special acts that benefit only the few of you. You refer to these as miracles because you know they work contrary to universal law. I hope you will understand that I give freedom to my children to make their own choices. I can't interfere in my children's lives. Each one feels that his cause is just. If I help one, the other becomes angry with me.

"I have supplied you with all things you need to lead a happy and peaceful life. If you use your intelligence to understand the way your universe works, and how you can cooperate with your brothers, you will increase the benefits for all of you beyond measure. But since you are already embroiled in a war, I'm afraid now you will have to allow events which each of your forces have set in motion to progress to their ultimate end. I love you all dearly. I fervently hope each of you survives."

As my frightened musings ended, I realized that silence had once more returned to the hold. The firing had ceased.

How long could we endure these terrifying episodes and still keep our sanity? How long could our lives last with no more food and water than they provided us? How long could our dying friends go on without medicines and treatment? Would there ever be an end to this journey in hell?

All of these unanswerable questions kept rolling out of my mind and I wondered to myself if I were in danger of losing my grip on reality. Was this trip going to be my undoing? I had been thinking a great deal about this problem and I felt certain it would help to talk it over with Liz. When I turned my head in his direction I could see that he had tipped his head back against the wall behind us. His eyes were closed, so I spoke to him quietly.

"Liz, can you talk?"

"Yeah, Murray."

"Can I bounce some ideas off you?"

"If it doesn't take long. I'm beat."

"Well, this voyage is beginning to push me to my limit. When firing starts on deck my heart begins to race and I feel as if I'm going to explode through my skin if the tension doesn't subside soon. I tend to think I'm the only prisoner affected so drastically, yet when I look at the faces of the guys around me I can see they must be experiencing the same terror that grips me. I'm convinced that we're all about drained of both energy and hope from these frequent threats of attack. Do you feel pretty much like that, too?"

"Pretty close, except that when it's all over I feel so damned depressed. I can't come out of it for several days, and I have a horrible headache that makes me sick to my stomach."

"I'm sorry, Liz. I should never have brought this up so soon. I…"

"No, no, it's okay. Might as well talk about it now as later. Maybe we'll both feel better if we go over it right away. Go ahead, Murray."

"Okay, but if at any time you don't want to go on any more, just say the word and we'll call it quits.

"Will do."

"What I've kinda been thinking about is this: Twice now since the trip began we have been scared out of our wits by the possibility of attack from our forces, right?"

"Right. Once when we arrived at the mouth of Davao Gulf, and then today just a short time ago."

"And during these two occasions did you ever really see any planes?"

"No, I can't say that I did."

"Did you hear anyone else say they had seen planes?"

"Not a soul."

"Then why do you suppose we reacted so quickly and so intensely?"

"God, I don't know. Probably because our airfield was bombed by our forces before we left. We know our planes can reach targets here in Mindanao, such as the one we're sitting in right now."

"And who else knows that?"

"Our guards and their officers."

"But do you think they are likely to make up the gun crews on this ship?"

"No, I doubt it. They're probably made up of men from the ship's crew, or men detached from other units and trained especially for that kind of duty. Good gun crews train as a team over a long period of time. They practice together every day. It's not a simple job."

"Right, I agree with you. So don't you think it makes sense that what we have experienced so far is probably two serious practice sessions, ordered on a sudden alert basis to test the gun crew's readiness for an emergency?"

"I guess that makes sense. So, you're saying that if we don't see some real evidence of our forces, we can probably assume we're not in any immediate danger. Right!"

"That's about it. Maybe it's too simple an answer, Liz, but I think we can reduce the wear and tear on our nerves by being more aware of what's happening—or not happening—whenever we hear gunfire. I need some way of dealing with these problems, or when we get to the end of our voyage they're going to carry me out of this filthy hell hole in a basket."

"Murray, I don't want to cut you off, but it's getting dark. I think a trip to the latrine cans is in order. Do you want to come along?"

"Sure, hang on. I'll be right with you."

In a moment or two we were on our way and luckily made it back just before last light. Both Liz and I were really ready to sleep. We exchanged good nights and called it a day.

On the fourth day, late in the afternoon, the rolling motion of our ship tapered off. After a short period of slow, smooth sailing, the vibration of the engines disappeared and we heard the rattling of the anchor chain as it left its housing and dropped into the water.

On the fifth day, when the Nips asked for volunteers to empty the latrine buckets, we arranged to get one or two men on deck who had served in southern Mindanao before the war. When they returned, they told us we had dropped anchor in the middle of Zamboanga Harbor. It had taken us four days to travel from the southeast corner of Mindanao to the southwest corner of the same island. All that day we sat without moving. The heat was devastating. Without motion there was no air flowing across the top of the hatch. The heat was sapping all our energy. All we could do is lie still and watch the rivulets of sweat coursing down our bodies. It was almost impossible to breathe, the air was so hot.

Day Six came and went. No change. Our ship didn't move. The same was true for Days Seven, Eight, Nine and Ten. This situation was truly critical. Even though the Japs selected our group because it represented the healthiest men in the main camp, it was a relative comparison. We could not favorably compare with healthy men who had not been prisoners for two and a half years. There was a limit to our endurance, especially under the conditions that were imposed on us. Many prisoners were ill and unable to care for themselves, and the stifling heat made even well men unable to function. If things didn't improve, many of us were going to die. As usual, I doubted the Japanese were at all concerned with that possibility.

Days Eleven, Twelve, Thirteen and Fourteen also passed and our ship still lay anchored in the harbor. Every prisoner had squirmed his way into a prone position, or as close as he could approximate it. No one moved. Saving energy and slowing breathing became first priority considerations for survival.

Liz turned toward me. His eyes were closed, his lips were dry and coated with a rim of dried froth that made it difficult for him to open his mouth to talk. "Murray...Murray, I don't think I'm going to make it...I...I feel so terribly tired. I think I'd...I'd just like to go to sleep...and not...wake up."

"Oh God, Liz...don't talk that way...don't let them break your spirit."

My eyes were filled with tears. I was sobbing uncontrollably with an over-powering grief.

"Liz, because our forces were surrendered they think we are weak and don't deserve to live. They don't value life; we do. We've got to show them that our way is better. We've got to live to show them we can do it no matter how difficult they make it. We've got to show them that we are stronger than they are."

All the time I was pleading with Liz I was softly wiping his face with a dirty old cloth I had been using to mop up my own sweat. I just wanted him to live. I held him securely in my arms for quite a long time while he slept, but I made sure I checked him every so often just to make sure he didn't give in to his desire for an endless sleep.

On Day Fifteen, about midmorning, the Japs lowered a ladder into the hold and ordered everyone to bring his belongings and come out of the hold. For an instant time seemed to come to a halt. Everyone was frozen momentarily in dis-belief. Then, when they became convinced they had really heard what they thought they had heard, they lunged toward the base of the ladder. Weaker men were pushed aside and even knocked down. The sight of 375 prisoners fighting each other to get up that ladder angered me intensely. Their only purpose was to get to the new place and grab what they considered the best location before anyone else could beat them to it.

Where were the defenders of the sick? Who would help them up the ladder with their pitiful little bundles of essentials? We were all in this together; why weren't we acting together? Was this the way "the survival of the fittest" works? It seemed more like the survival of the "feistiest" to me. I was really upset by this massive display of selfishness. I was so upset that I resolved to sit quietly where I was until all sick men had left the hold. I was going to be the last man up that ladder.

I soon regretted that decision when I realized that Liz had left already. First Jon and I became separated because I didn't wait for him; now Liz and I were lost to each other because he had not waited for me. I was overwhelmed with sadness. It was not likely that we would meet again wherever we were now being sent. Perhaps we might find each other at the end of our journey in Manila; I hoped so. Once again my idealism had cheated me out of a possible life-long friend. I berated myself for allowing a general concern for my fellow men to make me insensitive to the two men who were closest to me.

The Nips on deck now yelled down to those of us who were left in the hold, and especially to me, because I was making no effort to stand and at least look like I was planning to depart. I had no desire to anger them further so I got up and started to move toward the ladder. I wasn't the least bit sorry to leave this foul-smelling, waterborne oven. I couldn't see how anything ahead of us could be as bad as the fourteen days we had just endured on this hellish voyage. Little did I realize that what lay ahead would make these fourteen days seem like a pleasure cruise by comparison.

The *Shinyo Maru*

I climbed up the ladder and stepped down onto the deck. What a pleasure to leave that stinking atmosphere behind! Two of our guards from Lasang pointed in the direction they wanted me to go. It was then that I noticed another ship lying alongside ours only a few feet away. The name of that ship was the *Shinyo Maru*, a name I was destined to remember for the rest of my life.

A narrow plank stretched precariously across the gap between the two ships. I immediately felt a few moments of apprehension when I realized my next task was to get across that plank to the deck of the other ship. Our fourteen days in the hold had left us quite weak and unsure of our balance. When I reached the plank I hesitated a moment, took a deep breath, and strode deliberately forward with eyes looking straight ahead rather than down at the board and the water below. I made it across, but barely. I knew I was really lucky. If the distance had been much longer I might not have fared so well.

To my left, about 30 feet away, I saw the two men who had preceded me out of the hold. They both stood near a big open hatch!. Both of them dropped their small field bags down below so I walked up to the hatch, looked down, and couldn't believe my eyes. Suddenly I really regretted my choice of waiting so long! In this ship we weren't in the first section of the hold below deck. We were down at the extreme bottom of the ship.

Logo of the survivors of the Shinyo Maru

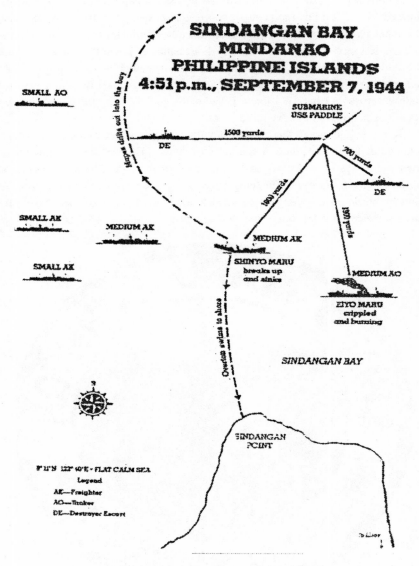

Diagram of the sinking of the Shinyo Maru

A narrow metal ladder ran all the way from the top deck to the keel below. It was the only way in and out of the hold. My God, if this ship was attacked by our planes the chances of our surviving were nonexistent. We'd never make it out of the hold. The thought of 500 men struggling to get up to the deck by climbing a small ladder that could accommodate only one man at a time left me both frightened and depressed. The top surface of the keel ran fore and aft through the entire compartment. The men below looked like miniatures rather than normal-sized humans. I dropped my field bag below and again followed the two men ahead until we reached the ladder. While I awaited my turn, I tried to determine what made the hold look so strange. A cargo hold is a very large open space within the body of a ship. This space is enclosed on each side by the hull of the ship and at front and back by walls, more commonly called bulkheads, of wood or metal. The deck encloses the top; the keel and lower hull of the ship seal the bottom. Usually in a medium-size ship such as the *Shinyo Maru*, the hold is divided into two sections. The upper section is about one-third of the total cargo space and the bottom section occupies the remaining two-thirds. A large square opening, or hatch, is placed in the floor at the center of the upper compartment. Directly above that hatch, one of similar dimensions is located on the main deck.

When the ship is loading, cargo booms on the ship swing over and pick up items from the dock, lift them up to the deck of the ship, and lower them through both hatches down into the bottom of the lower compartment. When the lower compartment is full, crew members cover the access hatch with boards and thereby seal off the bottom section of the hold. This also permits additional floor space in the upper section for more cargo. When the upper section is completely loaded, the deck hatch is closed with boards and sealed with canvas to protect the cargo below from any invasion of water.

In the ship we had just vacated, the access hatch to the lower hold was already sealed off. We were able, therefore, to occupy the entire floor area of the upper section. This was not true of the *Shinyo Maru*. In this ship we were destined to occupy the bottom of the lower compartment.

Another unusual feature of the *Shinyo Maru* involved the location of the two hatches. The place where I was standing, awaiting my turn to go down into the hold, was very narrow. The bulkhead which arose behind me formed the front of the ship's super-structure. This same wall continued down to the very bottom of the ship and formed the rear of the hold. This meant that the hatch was set near the rear of the hold, not at the center. It looked as if some giant hand had pulled the upper section hatch toward the rear of the ship until its near edge was just short of the rear wall of the hold. Thus, in the upper compartment there were two cargo platforms on each side of the ship and one across the front bulkhead; but none at the rear where I was standing. This strange arrangement, however, permitted the permanent attachment of the long, metal ladder I was waiting to descend. So it was that as I stared into the entire hold for the first time, I was looking through two framed openings at a very large compartment beneath them both, a compartment which to me seemed destined to become a giant tomb.

As I began my descent down the ladder I could see very large bales of cargo tied with new, two-inch manila ropes filling the upper compartment. Continuing on down to the bottom compartment, I realized how much larger it appeared. It must have been at least two or three times deeper than the upper compartment. After what seemed like an eternity I stepped from the ladder to the keel of the ship. As I turned to face my fellow POWs I was discouraged to find that there was no place for me to sit. Everybody was jammed together at the bottom and there were now 500 of us in this hold and 250 in another. Apparently this hold had last been used to carry bulk cement and each man was sitting in a foot or more of the gray stuff. It probably felt very comfortable at the moment, but I wondered how their skin would be affected when they began to sweat again.

Ahead of me I saw a big piece of granite which had been lashed to the keel to provide ballast for the ship; there were two men sitting on it. They motioned to me, indicating that apparently they estimated there was enough room for a third person on their perch. So I walked over, thanked them profusely, and sat down next to my new companions.

There wasn't enough room for each of us to lie down at the same time, and we didn't know how many more days remained before our trip would end. We learned by experimenting that if one man sat erect with his legs drawn up under his chin, a second man could lie down behind the first man with his legs dangling over the side of the rock, and the third man could lie with his upper body across the thighs of the second man and his legs also hanging over the side of the rock. We all agreed to that routine and took turns so each of us could get some rest.

Later that same morning of the fifteenth day, the Japs began to lower the latrine buckets again. With 500 of us in the hold now, the adjustments to make room for the buckets approached chaos. After much bickering and flaring of tempers, necessary changes were made and peace was restored, at least temporarily.

We sensed from the vibrations of our ship that we were underway again and would soon be leaving Zamboanga Harbor. When it was my turn to lie down I looked up at the top hatch and realized our rock perch was just about dead center below that opening, but a long, long way below. I realized I couldn't go on worrying about the gravity of our situation. Sure, it was obvious that we didn't stand a chance of survival if this ship were attacked, but it seemed wiser to me to concentrate on the passage of time. If we reached our destination safely, and soon, we would not have to be concerned about survival. I don't think the majority of prisoners shared my outlook, however. Their eyes seemed constantly glued to the top hatch opening and their gaunt faces and worried appearance reflected their fear of the future.

On the sixteenth day, things progressed about as usual except that we were getting awfully weary. The heat was getting to us. We had streams of perspiration pouring from our bodies all the time. The depth of our position was such that not much cooling air reached us. We had not been provided with adequate water since the trip began. The lack of nourishing food was taking its toll. Our bodies had long ago been drained of any fat reserves and we were getting that skin-over-skeleton look so characteristic of starving people. To add to our worries, the Nips came to the edge of the hatch opening and called for men to empty the latrine buckets. Because of the increased number of men in the hold and the greater distance from the floor of the hold to the top, they called for more deck workers. This time when they hauled the buckets up, the tremendous distance made it worse than before. The pails were swinging wildly from one side of the hold to the other. It was indeed fortunate if any of the contents got to the top.

We continued this ritual daily and again, despite its despicable side effects, it proved to have a satisfying end. When the men returned to their places in the hold, they told us we were now part of a nine-ship convoy and we were still sailing relatively close to shore. This was good news. Being a part of a nine-ship convoy seemed much safer than sailing alone.

On the seventeenth day, shortly past noon, the guards above placed a board across the hatch opening just where the ladder reached the deck. Although it was done rather quietly, the move did not escape the attention of the men whose position enabled them to see the opening above. Each man who saw the placement instantly sat up straight and fully alert, watching to see if more boards would follow. To our great horror, the Japs continued putting the boards across the hatch, cutting off all the light and all the air from us. Many prisoners were standing now and called in frightened, quavering voices to the soldiers above, "Hey, stop! Stop! We won't be able to breathe down here. What are you trying to do, kill us all!"

But the march of boards across the hatch continued on.

They had covered more than half the hatch now. I felt terrified at what was happening. My heart was pounding at the base of my neck. I felt as if an electric current had been loosed in my mouth and I experienced a strange metallic taste on my tongue. A surge of panic was rising in my body and I knew that I was on the verge of screaming at the top of my lungs.

At that moment two men who could stand the tension no longer leaped up from the floor and started to plunge across the bodies in the bottom of the hold. They were running for the ladder. They got to the bottom and started to climb toward the top, but men seated next to the ladder reached up, grabbed them and hauled them back down. Then they cradled them in their arms and rocked them back and forth, just as you would a little child. They were sobbing beyond control.

The Japanese stopped one board from the end of the hatch, so we had left just a tiny shaft of light, and only a whisper of air to breathe. I was afraid they would add the last board, then cover all the boards with canvas and lash them down with ropes. That would really mark the end of all of us.

On the eighteenth day when we awoke, still feeling the terror of the day before, the boards were unchanged. Our despair was evident. Each man's head was bowed down on his chest. We were almost at the point of completely giving up hope. We couldn't understand how we were going to make it through this impossible ordeal. My body felt as if it were welded into one piece. I was as rigid as a board. I could hardly breathe.

It was then that I made a decision that I had never had to make before. I realized that despite my longing to return home to my parents, my sister, and to Fee in particular, there was a very great possibility that I might die right here on this ship. Tears welled up in my eyes and rolled down my cheeks. I was determined not to give up but I also felt it was foolish to deny the reality that lay before me.

At that moment one of our Catholic chaplains, Father Joseph Le Fleur, stood up in the darkness of the hold and asked to be permitted to hold just a short service for everyone, asking God to grant us strength to endure whatever lay ahead of us. Chaplain Le Fleur was a marvelous man. I had talked to him many times in camp and I admired him so much. His calm, clear voice enriched by the addition of an Acadian French accent, brought solace to us all as if we were hearing the very voice of God himself. I was deeply moved and resolved to search again for the possibility of hope in our future, even though it might be only a glimmer.

The next day, the nineteenth day of our voyage, at about five o'clock in the afternoon we heard machine gun fire on the deck, voices yelling—nothing new. It was my turn to sit up while my two friends rested. Because I could hear no sound of attacking planes, I knew the Jap gun crew was having a practice alert again. Nevertheless, I put my head down on my knees and began to pray. That prayer, although started, was never finished.

The Paddle

In the early afternoon of August 22, 1944, just two days after our prison ship sailed from Davao Gulf, the United States Submarine Paddle left Fremantle, Western Australia and headed out into the Indian Ocean on its fifth war patrol. Commander B.H. Nowell, Captain—a veteran of seven previous war patrols— and Lt. Commander J.P. Fitzpatrick, Executive Officer and Navigator, plotted Paddle's course north through the clutter of small Southeast Asian islands and stealthily maneuvered her into Philippine waters. Paddle's mission: to attack enemy shipping in the East Sulu Sea. On the 6th of September, Captain Nowell wrote in his log: "Surfaced. Underway on surface, patrolling coast {of Mindanao} and headed for Sindangan Point."

At 1520 hours on September 7, while patrolling submerged, Nowell sighted smoke rising from the western side of the Point. He immediately placed Paddle on course to the suspect area.

At 1613 he sighted masts and stacks of three large ships.

At 1637, just 24 minutes later, he had in view a nine-ship convoy moving northwest toward Sindangan Point.

An escort vessel preceded the group followed by a tanker and two medium-size freighters. All sailed very close to the coast line. A second escort patrolled the rear of this formation. Two small freighters, a small tanker and a third escort trailed somewhat behind the initial element.

Acting quickly, the Captain calculated his target options and then decided to make his initial approach on the tanker, since in his judgment it was the most valuable ship in the convoy. As he put Paddle in attack position, the periscope revealed the forward escort moving across his line of vision no more than 300 yards away.

At 1651 Paddle lurched slightly as each of four torpedoes whined out of its tube and careened toward the unsuspecting tanker. Sonar bearings verified that all charges were running on course. Captain Nowell instantly called for a shift in Paddles's position, then sent two additional torpedoes hurtling toward the lead freighter. Rapidly rotating the periscope back to the tanker, he witnessed the first of two hits. In only a matter of moments now the escort vessels would be charging down on Paddle's position. He swung the periscope back to pick up the closest escort. On the way he caught sight of two highly visible torpedo wakes heading directly for the lead freighter. As he brought the escort in focus he could see she was bearing straight for Paddle at attack speed. "Go deep! Go deep!" he yelled to Control. He pressed his head close against the periscope watching the escort's frenzied approach. Just before the periscope sliced below the surface—only 59 seconds after firing the sixth torpedo—two timed hits were heard slamming into the lead freighter!

HEADQUARTERS ARMY SERVICE FORCES
OFFICE OF THE PROVOST MARSHAL GENERAL
WASHINGTON 25, D. C.

1 May 1944

Mrs. Richard Sneddon,
653 West Glenoaks Boulevard, Apt. #2,
Glendale 2, California.

Dear Mrs. Sneddon:

The Provost Marshal General directs me to reply to your letter of 18 April 1944 regarding your son, Second Lieutenant Murray M. Sneddon.

Verification of the records in this office indicates that your son is interned as a prisoner of war by the Japanese Government in the Philippine Islands. This office has received no information which would indicate that your son is dead. It is believed that the magazine article is an error.

Sincerely yours,

Howard F. Bresee,
Colonel, C.M.P.,
Assistant Director,
Prisoner of War Division.

Letter to Mrs. Richard Sneddon, May 1, 1944

Chapter 10

Survival
and Escape

At the instant Paddle's two torpedoes slammed into our hold, I lost consciousness. Somewhere down in the depths of that stricken ship I hung in limbo, hovering between life and death. I really don't know what happened. However, a friend who claimed he remained conscious during the entire experience told me the following story, which I describe to you now in my own words.

When the torpedoes exploded against the hull of the *Shinyo Maru*, the lives of many of our fellow prisoners suddenly, and very violently, ended. Water began to enter the hold. From the point where the torpedo struck the forward hold, a jagged fracture raced along that part of the ship's hull that extended below the water line, and then the hull wrenched apart. A torrent of water gushed into the hold with tremendous power. In only a moment we were covered with thirty feet of water.

Prior to the entry of the water, many of the giant packing cases that were stored in the upper compartment toppled over and came tumbling down, crushing the men below. The entire forward wall of the hold, which was made of wood, collapsed over the prisoners sitting in front of it, instantly killing many and trapping others to drown as the hold filled with water. To make the chaos even worse, soldiers on deck began to lob grenades into the hold to ensure that none of us could get out."

During my first conscious moment, I opened my eyes and saw a strange, yellow light in front of me. Within that yellow field I could see darker forms, but they all appeared so soft and vague that I was unable to tell what they were. Later, I came to the conclusion that the yellow light was sunlight shining through sea water tainted with cement dust; and some of the things that bumped into me were probably bodies, or body parts, of many of my fellow *Pows*.

I was floating under the water, pushed by the in-rushing current, bumping and being bumped by things I was unable to identify. Quite suddenly my head broke above the surface of the water and I realized for the first time what had happened. The very thing I had dreaded for so long had come to pass. I was float- ing around in the hold of a rapidly sinking ship and there wasn't much time left to get out.

When my head first broke above the water, I was facing into a rear corner of the hold. Not more than three feet above my head I saw the under side of the upper compartment floor. I could see it steadily moving down on top of me. Fearing the worst, I whirled around and swam as fast as I could out into the open area beneath the two hatches. I wanted to stay in that area, but found it impossible.

The water moved powerfully in a large clockwise circle that flowed around the entire hold. I couldn't free myself from its control no matter how hard I tried. Then, just ahead of me, I saw one of the pipes that supported the inner edge of the deck above, so I quickly reached out and grabbed it. As I hung on, I had a chance to look around and take stock of my situation. I saw that the hold was more than two-thirds filled with water, but where were my fellow prisoners? Five hundred men were jammed into this hold—where were they? I saw no one—not a single soul. How long was I unconscious? Could they have gotten out before me? I prayed that might be the case.

I looked up to the hatch above. It was fully open. The boards that covered it were blown away by the explosive power of the torpedoes. What a relief that was!. But, what about the ladder? It was there, but useless. Judging by the water level in the hold, the ship's front end was under water and was listing strongly to the left. Since the ladder was permanently fixed to the ship, it too was leaning to the left and the top was leaning forward. I knew it would be impossible for me to keep my feet on the ladder while climbing. I didn't feel I could go up by hand, one rung at a time, with my feet hanging in space. I was sure I didn't have strength available for such an effort.

During the time I made these observations, I had to move my hand positions several times farther up the pipe. I noted that the water was rising fast. It occurred to me that all I would have to do was be patient and the water would soon lift me to the deck hatch above. As simple as this reasoning seemed, I feared it contained one marked flaw. Even before the water reached the top, it was very likely the ship would be heading for the bottom. So I decided to wait until I was about twelve feet from the deck; then I would try to climb the pipe to the open hatch above. One thing I was very sure of: I didn't want to get trapped in that ship as it started its final plunge to the bottom of the sea. The thought terrified me.

The time to make my exit attempt was at hand. My heart was pounding wildly, my mouth was bone dry, and I was shaking with fear. I wondered if my wet body could cling to the metal pipe, or would it slide right back after each try. There was no time to ponder that question; it was now or never. I grasped the pipe with both my arms and legs and began to climb. I really felt the weakness that had taken over my body after nineteen days in the hold. I struggled to overcome that weakness, but my remaining strength was ebbing fast. My fear told me I was not going to make it, but thinking about the other choice charged me with new energy.

I finally reached the retaining wall around the hatch. My supreme test was at hand. I clung to the pipe for a minute or two more, then I tried to throw one leg up until I hooked my heel over the edge of the hatch. Finally, after several tries, I made it. I decided then to wait no longer. I was tiring fast, so with every last bit of strength I could muster I pulled my body up and over the hatch and onto the deck.

Because of my sudden, all-out effort, my momentum caused me to overrotate and I fell toward the deck on my back. I expected to meet the hard surface of the deck, but was surprised when I contacted a softer, more yielding surface. I quickly rolled over to my hands and knees and was shocked to see I had fallen directly on top of a Japanese soldier. His face was badly burned. Large, black pieces of skin hung loosely from his cheeks. For an instant I saw him only as an enemy and was ready to fight for my survival, but I felt much better when I realized the explosion had relieved me of the effort. He was dead.

I suddenly became aware that this momentary diversion had taken my attention away from my surroundings. It was very possible that at this very moment some Nip soldier was sighting down the barrel of his rifle with me as the target. A flash of fear brought me quickly to life. I dropped flat on my stomach and swept my eyes over the deck and the wheel house beyond, but I saw no one. The only Jap soldiers I saw were all dead ones.

I did notice rhythmic patches of steam rising from the ship's whistle, but the sound seemed to be coming from miles away. I suspected at that moment that my hearing had been damaged by the explosion within the hold, because even loud sounds very near to me seemed quite muffled. If I could reach shore safely, would I be able to avoid the Japs? My life depended on my ability to hear them coming.

The bow of the ship was well below the water and listing to the left. I got a clear view to the open ocean from where I crouched. I saw the other ships of our convoy scattering in every direction to avoid being hit. Two Jap planes attempted to bomb the escaping submarine, but without depth charges I doubted they would be successful.

I diverted my attention to the inclined deck to my right. As I began to crawl on all fours up the 15 or 20-degree slope, I noticed that the solid railing that enclosed the deck had sheared off at a point directly ahead of me and dropped into the sea. When I got closer to the edge of the deck, I saw a large land mass about two and one-half miles away. Its low foothills were heavily forested right down to the edge of a narrow, sandy beach. To my left I saw an oil tanker that also had been hit by the submarine that attacked us. Her captain ran her up to the shore to keep her from sinking.

Large ocean swells moved diagonally across my field of vision; they headed directly for the tanker. Many men who tried to swim from our position to the beach straight ahead found themselves forced into the vicinity of that tanker. Just as I was about to divert my eyes elsewhere, a lone figure rose up out of the water and began to stagger up the beach. Instantly a cloud of dust and sand enveloped him. When the dust had cleared I saw him lying dead on the sand, killed by a hail of bullets from a Jap machine gun on the tanker.

Looking to the right, I witnessed a sight that made me recoil in fear. No more than 25 feet from me I saw a life boat suspended about 30 feet in the air, dangling by its launching ropes. Four Jap soldiers lowered it to its present position, but now it refused to be lowered any further. If they managed to launch it, none of us would get to shore alive.

Two of the soldiers, the ones at each end, hacked frantically at the ropes, hoping to release the stranded boat. One was using a bayonet, the other a saber. The other two soldiers, the ones in the center, were firing their rifles at any American POWS they could see, but particularly those who were heading for the shore.

Directly below me, grouped tightly against our ship, a mixed collection of Japanese soldiers and American POWs were clinging to bits of wreckage. From my vantage point on the deck above them, they appeared to be randomly grouped into clusters of two to four men. A five-foot circle of unoccupied water had temporarily opened up in this random grouping, and this was a fortunate opportunity for me.

When the soldiers in the life boat stopped to reload, I quickly started walking down the side of the ship until I couldn't go any farther without jumping. Then I plummeted down to the water. I don't know what the distance to the water might have measured; I only know that as I hurtled down I had that sinking feeling that made me wonder if my fall would ever end. Although I didn't have much time to gauge my leap, I managed to hit the spot for which I'd aimed. I plunged

Japanese shooting at escaping prisoners from beached tanker

down some 10 or 12 feet and felt the sudden sting of the water as it was driven up my nose. Then I kicked vigorously to propel myself to the top.

When my head broke the surface of the water, I wiped my eyes quickly and found myself looking straight at one of the prisoners who slept in the bay across from mine at Lasang. I always enjoyed talking to him and considered him a real fine and intelligent person. More to build my own confidence than anything else, I spoke his name. His only reply was, "I'm shot." I looked at him more carefully and noticed a small red mark on his left chest just a few inches below his collarbone.

He was clinging to a worn, four-foot piece of wood. As the current moved him about he slowly rotated until his back was facing me. Then it became clear to me that he didn't have a chance to reach shore alive. The bullet, as it passed through his body, expanded and blew a three-inch hole in his back as it came out. I could see the shattered edge of his shoulder blade and on into his chest. Some of his friends were trying to help him hang on to the piece of wood, but he kept slipping off. Even with the best of medical help it is unlikely that he could be saved, but in our predicament his life would end soon.

My mind flooded with sadness. What a tragedy! How can mankind permit this to happen to such a fine person? He survived the torpedoing only to be shot in the water two and one-half miles from freedom. All the other men in this small group were in a similar state. Many were seriously wounded and most were unable to swim. The Japanese in this group appeared to be in shock: Their charred faces were black, their eyes fixed and empty -looking. I knew I need not be concerned with any of them so far as my personal safety was concerned; but the lifeboat—that problem really worried me a great deal.

Because I had picked a moment when the soldiers in the lifeboat were completely occupied with their own concerns, I don't think they were really aware that I had jumped into the water. I stayed very close to that tight little group of men next to the ship so I would not be singled out. I made it a point also to work my way through the group, little by little, whenever the soldiers were not looking in our direction. My intention was to reach a point nearer the bow of the ship where the curvature of the hull concealed me from their view.

By watching the four Japanese soldiers carefully, I did manage to carry out that maneuver. I felt much safer farther away from their area. I frequently inched forward a bit so I could check on their progress. I was very uneasy about my location. If the ship, without warning, began to make its final plunge I was in a very risky position. Also I was concerned about the time; evening was approaching and I had a long swim ahead of me. As I was carefully sneaking a look at the lifeboat, I noticed that the soldier who was hacking at his rope with the saber, had speeded up his effort. I figured perhaps he was nearly through his rope and was now eager to finish it off.

This must have been the case, for a few minutes later the rope did part and his end of the boat began to drop down. I held my breath in anticipation. If the rope at the other end was sufficiently severed, the weight of the lifeboat might cause that rope also to break. In that event, it would be possible for them to successfully launch their boat. However, as it happened, the rope on the other end held fast.

All four soldiers had only an instant to leap clear of their falling boat before it abruptly stopped in a vertical position. Fortunately for us, they were primarily concerned at that moment with their own safety. They had let go of their weapons and all of them, men and weapons, were flung into the sea. That was the moment I had been waiting for. My chance for freedom had arrived. I moved away from the *Shinyo Maru* and began to swim. I knew I didn't want to swim straight in to shore. I wanted to avoid that tanker at all costs. I noticed that the crew of the tanker had just successfully launched two lifeboats. They were now picking up American POWs and Japanese soldiers who had drifted into the tanker's vicinity.

We later learned that Denver Rose, one of our survivors, was among the men picked up by the Japanese. They tied his hands behind his back in such a way that he was also attached to the fantail railing of the tanker. Twenty-nine other American POWS were similarly tied. Then, starting at one end of the line, the Nips began to execute the recaptured prisoners. As each man was killed, they dumped his body overboard.

Denver was the fourth man in line. As soon as the first prisoner was executed, he worked frantically to sever his rope by rubbing it against a rough, frayed part of the cable he was secured to. When his hands were free, he ran at top speed toward the front part of the ship. Because his escape was so unexpected, the Nips were caught by surprise. He got quite a head start on the soldiers who pursued him. When he reached the bow of the ship, he hid in a hole through which the anchor chain passed. When the soldiers reached his area, they thought he had jumped overboard. After searching the waters below without success, they gave up and returned to the fantail of the ship to continue the executions. When darkness settled over the area, Denver crawled down the anchor chain and made it to shore. He was the only survivor of the 30-man group.

I was afraid to stay in the area near the *Shinyo Maru*. When the other ships that were scattered out to sea came back, I knew what they would do. I had been witness to sufficient examples to be convinced that they did not intend that any of us should be left alive. So I decided to swim parallel to the shoreline, and try to come in on the far side of a point of land I could see to the west. That course required me to swim the entire length of the *Shinyo Maru* and on into the distance away from the tanker.

I soon confirmed my estimate of the sea's power. The ocean swells were steadily pushing me toward shore. I used a side-stroke as I swam: This kept my head and shoulders well down in the water. The scissors kick kept me moving steadily without sending up a geyser of water to betray my position. By stopping to rest occasionally, I was able to look back at the *Shinyo Maru* and then to my destination, to see how much headway I was making. I became more and more concerned about my progress and soon realized I was not going to get around the point; I was going to lose the protection I was hoping for. I tried to increase my pace but my efforts to get out of the *Shinyo Maru* had left me to too weak and tired. I hated to do it, but I had to give up that effort and take a chance that I could still get to shore successfully. I did discover a small piece of three-inch diameter bamboo drifting in the water. It contained only one watertight cell, but it did give me a little buoyancy, which saved some energy for me.

When I next rested, I looked back at the *Shinyo Maru* and noticed her attitude in the water had greatly changed. It was obvious she was about to go down. The forward section was completely under water all the way back to the beginning of the super-structure. The stern was high in the air when she began to slowly glide down into the sea. When the water hit the boilers, clouds of steam arose momentarily, then she plunged silently toward the bottom. When all traces of her stern had disappeared below the surface of the water, a strange thing occurred.

The water surrounding the site suddenly began to rise like a huge bulge. Actually it was the upper surface of a large bubble which was inflated by a number of pockets of air still trapped in the ship. The change in position of *Shinyo Maru* as it plunged toward the bottom permitted these various reservoirs of air to escape and form one giant balloon. When the bubble surfaced it burst, the air escaped, and the water subsided to its normal level.

I turned around and began to swim. I wondered if the group of men I had recently left had been able to survive the ship's plunge. I also wondered, sadly, how many POWs had been carried down and were now entombed in the depths of her holds. I was grateful I was able to put a little distance between me and her position before the sinking occurred, but I still had a long way to go.

I began to swim again. Then, suddenly, I was startled by strong rumbling and clashing sounds that slowly dissipated over a period of several minutes. Because I couldn't locate the source of this sound, it really frightened me. I swept the sea with my eyes but could see nothing. Then I realized that sound carries exceptionally well in water. What I heard, and felt, was the *Shinyo Maru* settling on the rocks below. As I was turning back to resume my swim I saw little spurts of water rising in a sharp line in front of me, and almost simultaneously I barely made out the muffled rattle of a machine gun from the fantail of the tanker.

I went under fast and stayed under until I couldn't hold my breath any longer. Then I came up on my back so only my face was exposed above the water. I took in deep breaths of air and waited a while before attempting to swim again. I had been careless when searching for the possible origin of the sound I heard, and some Nip gunner on the tanker picked up my movements. That was a close call. I vowed to be more careful from then on. Unfortunately I had to dive under several more times when swimmers beyond my position, but aligned with mine, were detected, thereby putting me in jeopardy.

The torpedoing of the *Shinyo Maru* took place shortly after 5:00 p.m. and now daylight was fading. Unfortunately, the cross current pushed me much too quickly toward the shore and I saw that I would reach land in the most exposed place, the point, and at the worst time, before dark. Because the beach area and surf all the way to the point were within range of the machine guns on the beached tanker, I would have to be especially careful to stay down in the water and remain hidden until after dark. Then and only then could I dare to venture on shore and move around the point.

As I neared the shore I felt much more keenly the powerful force of the ocean swells. They lifted me up and pushed me forward, then raced on ahead, leaving me to slide back into the trough behind. I was no match for the energy they exerted. They carried me forward at a hectic pace. I could veer to one side or the other but could not stop, even for a moment, to check what lay ahead. I wanted to approach the shore with caution but was being driven there pell-mell. Soon I caught sight of the rolling tops of the swells as they began to break into waves. Beyond that point I also spotted chunks of jagged rock rising just above the surface of the water. In the faint back-light of twilight they appeared coal-black. Yet, at times, water surged over them so completely that they were buried in a snowy -white blanket of tumbling foam.

My mind began to process the various bits and pieces of information I had seen and felt on the way in. Those rocks looked menacing. If the tide swept me into them with much force, I could be badly cut up. On the other hand, they offered excellent cover if I could just hang onto them until complete darkness developed. I started to veer toward the right of the highest rock mass I could see. The tanker was to my left. That was the direction from which I expected any machine gun fire to come.

When I reached the line of breakers, I found myself completely immersed in foam and tumbling water. I expected at any moment to be raked over the top of a low-lying rock outcropping but luck was with me. I continually used my forward momentum to move to the right side of the chunk of rock I had selected earlier. One final surge and I reached the vicinity of my intended goal. I thrust out my arms stiffly in front of me, partly to hold my body away from the rocks and partly to find the sturdiest handholds available.

The instant my hands made contact I knew the fading light had deprived me of some important information. This was not a mass of rock I was clinging to; it was a living community of coral. Cuts from coral can easily become infected, but common sense suggested to me that the threat of infected cuts did not seem too important when compared to the damage inflicted by a hail of machine gun bullets. In reality the coral made an excellent hiding place for me since it jutted above the water more than the height of my head.

I hung onto my living anchor, waiting for sufficient darkness to develop so I could attempt to go ashore. Several times strong surges of surf battered my body against the sharp surface, but I managed to maintain my grip, so the location of my cover remained secure. Twice machine gun fire was directed down the shoreline from the tanker, but I felt protected in my temporary hiding place.

I grew anxious now to go ashore, and I felt the risk of being seen was minimal. At the next shoreward surge of the water I let go of my handholds and started to move toward the beach. In a short time I found the water calmer and my feet began to drop down until I felt the sandy bottom. I continued walking, with bent legs, in order to keep my upper body under the water. Then I crawled forward on hands and knees until I left the water and started up the beach. Wanting to move quickly around the point to my right, I stood up and started to walk.

As I made my first step, my legs crumpled beneath me and I promptly fell forward to the sand. I tried four times to walk and fell each time. It was imperative that I move around the point; it was necessary for my own safety. So I tried a new approach. I rose to my feet but made no attempt to walk. I just stood there shaking and wobbling, trying to maintain my balance. My strength was about gone. After what seemed like an eternity I began to feel like I was getting the hang of this business of standing. So I ventured one step, then stopped for a few moments. After repeating this approach several times I began to feel my circulation improving. My confidence also improved a great deal and I began to walk along the beach and around the point.

Once around the point I was able to make out the dim shapes of several other POWs who had arrived on shore about the same time as I did. Before I moved in their direction, I began a quick check to see what injuries, if any, I had sustained.

The left side of my head was really swollen, probably due to the knockout blow I received when the torpedoes first struck the ship. My eardrums had been shattered by the power of the explosion. Blood was running out both my ears and coursing down each side of my neck. My chest was bleeding from the many times the surf had slammed me into the coral patch I was clinging to, and later I learned that, while still in the ship, grenade fragments had penetrated my lower legs. Yet, taking all things into consideration, I had fared well—no broken bones, no bullet wounds—and best of all, I was still alive.

I began to move toward the nearest man. He noticed my approach and seemed to be waiting for me to reach his position before continuing on. When I was about two steps from him he turned and started to walk. As we walked quietly together we could see the other men moving in our direction. Soon all six of us converged into a tight circle, and someone immediately introduced the question that was on all our minds.

"Do any of you have any idea where we are?"

Although the voice had spoken in low tones, I was instantly reminded that my hearing had been seriously impaired. I could hardly hear. I was so thankful to be with others who could. I didn't want to die after getting this far toward freedom.

In response to the question, a couple of men shook their heads from side to side and others replied with a simple "No." We didn't know what island we were on, or if there were villages nearby…or if Japanese soldiers might be in the area. We knew that the Nips on the tanker could easily put a patrol on shore, and it was of paramount importance to us to distance ourselves from that area as quickly as possible. All agreed that we should continue down the beach, so we walked quietly, and as quickly as we were physically able, away from the scene of the torpedoing.

We really hadn't covered a great distance when we found ourselves stopped by a huge rock formation about 30 feet high which extended several hundreds of feet across the sand and out into the ocean. The water was choppy and rough all around the base of the outcropping and none of us wanted to chance a swim around that hazardous-looking barrier. There was still a faint blush of twilight over the distant horizon and as we had made our way along the beach I kept thinking we were probably clearly silhouetted against that narrow band of light. In my fearful state it was easy for me to imagine Nip riflemen lurking in the dense brush above the sand. Fortunately, my companions decided to move up through the brush to see what lay beyond the beach.

The going was difficult because night had finally settled over us and the sky, although filled with a myriad of stars above, was pitch-black right down to the horizon. No light radiated into the dense cover of trees through which we were passing. It seemed foolish to fumble on blindly. When we found ourselves moving through a large patch of tall grass, which could provide good cover, we quickly decided to bed down there for a while until the moon came up. We remained there for all of two minutes. By that time we were being attacked by swarms of mosquitoes.

We came stumbling out of the grass, flailing our arms around wildly in an attempt to rid ourselves of this new menace, but not daring to make a sound. None of us was wearing much more than a Japanese G-string, so the mosquitoes were having a field day at our expense. Under other circumstances it could have seemed comical, but now we were trying desperately to avoid drawing attention to our location. Once free of the mosquitoes we dropped down in a crouch and quietly listened for any sounds that might indicate that our presence had been discovered. We heard only silence.

We arose slowly, held our positions for a moment, then proceeded to move ahead cautiously. The moon was just rising and our surroundings were becoming more visible. Twice we heard a dog barking in the distance—probably a village, but inhabited by whom? We didn't want to take chances, so we steered a course that would keep us at a substantial distance from that sound.

In a short while we found ourselves in a grove of banana trees—no fruit, unfortunately—but a trail ran through it and disappeared into the distance. Walking on the trail with our bare feet was a pleasant change from the heavy brush and rocky hillside we had traversed since we left the beach. Then, suddenly, we were paralyzed with fear when we saw a silhouetted figure walking toward us on the trail ahead.

We froze instantly, not daring to move. Every man was trying to read that silhouette. I couldn't see anything resembling the shape of a rifle. There was no saber dangling from his waist. He seemed to be barefoot. I was ready to bet he was a Filipino. He hadn't seen us yet, so we had an advantage over him if he turned hostile. When he got within speaking distance one of our men called out, "Hey, friend, where are you going?"

He stopped dead in his tracks, trying to make out the location of the person who spoke to him. Then, as he saw all of us, he began to talk excitedly and pointed back down the trail in the direction from which he had come. To our disadvantage, however, he spoke no English. He continued to talk rapidly and repeatedly pointed in the direction he seemed to want us to go. This called for a quick conference.

He was obviously Filipino. He seemed friendly and we could do with some help. It must have startled him to come across six nearly naked Americans, bloody and disheveled, walking through a banana grove in the middle of the night. We decided to trust him, but to be in a state of readiness to act if he seemed to be leading us into an ambush. We motioned to him to lead the way and we fell into line behind him.

I was not conscious of the time we followed the Filipino. Because of the fears brought on by my lack of hearing, I closely examined the type of terrain we were passing through. I feared that this area, or that one, presented an obvious threat to our lives. It seemed to me we were taking a big risk, trusting a man whose language we couldn't understand. So when we ultimately arrived at a small nipa hut, probably our intended destination, it came as a surprise to me that we had arrived here so quickly.

The door of the hut was completely open and the room beyond was illuminated by the soft orange glow of a single tiny candle. We could see a small figure seated at a table near the center of the room. Our guide was extending one arm toward the opening and with the other was motioning here to us to enter. We were hesitant for obvious reasons. This could be a trap. We cautiously approached to a point where we could see more of the interior. There was no one but the single figure visible in the room, so hesitantly and fearfully we entered. The person seated at the table was a young boy, maybe fourteen or fifteen years old. As we entered he looked up at us, then broke into a broad, beautiful smile. He stood up, and in perfect English said, "Oh, sirs. We are so glad to see you. We have been looking for you. We have your supper ready."

I felt the pent-up stress of all 19 days of our miserable and terrifying voyage, and the years of imprisonment before it, bleeding from my body like air from a pricked balloon. My long-constricted muscles, which had held my scrawny frame in rigid readiness for the next trauma slowly began to relax and I felt a

great weariness consume my entire mind and body. I was dead tired, but happy
beyond description.

My fellow survivors had experienced a similar transformation, I was sure.
Their faces, which had been haggard and gaunt, were now smiling. Yet there
were furrowed brows above the smiles that attested to the memories that were
still alive within each of us. For a few, they would dissipate and finally disappear;
for most of us they would never leave, but haunt us for the rest of our lives.

Filipino offering banana to wounded escapee

Our young host quickly passed plates to us, and from a covered container behind him he served us generous helpings of cooked cracked corn. This form of corn would normally be used to feed chickens, but the Japanese had confiscated every grain of rice they could find, including next year's seed rice. Everyone in the village was eating cracked corn. They were generously serving us a very precious commodity upon which their own lives depended. The young man informed us that they heard the explosions when the ship was hit; they saw and heard the planes overhead, and were aware of the ship's plaintive whistle trying to summon help. However the presence of rifle and machine gun fire prompted them to remain away from the beach for a while. But when the first American survivors began to reach shore, they sent out villagers to guide them to safety. They were fed quickly at the collection points, then escorted back into the hills to recover.

Our young host also informed us that we were still on the island of Mindanao. We had traversed only about half the island's contour in our 19-day voyage. We learned, too, that it was his village, the village of Liloy, that was bravely giving us help in spite of the possibility of retaliation by the Japanese. We thanked him profusely for their help, and since we were now finished eating, we were promptly moved on to the final collection area several miles into the hills beyond us.

The moonlight enabled us to find our destination well before dawn, but we were confused when we first got there. We could see no one because of the high, dense growth of brush in front of us. Then our guides moved forward quickly and held some of the limbs and foliage back in one area so we could pass through. On the other side we entered a broad, grassy slope which climbed to the rear of a well-sheltered, but unoccupied, Filipino home. The entire yard was surrounded by a wall of high brush. It was certainly an excellent place of concealment.

Survivors were sleeping soundly all around us, so after a whispered thank you to our guides we moved quietly to an unoccupied area and collapsed on the grass like dead men. I felt as if I could sleep forever. Before I fell asleep I uttered a short prayer, thanking God for giving us the strength to complete our first step toward freedom. Then I closed my eyes and instantly left this world and all its cares behind.

For most of the next two days I drifted in and out of consciousness. For brief moments I awoke and talked with other survivors. The conversations always followed the same pattern. Everyone asked for information about close friends: "Were they near you on the ship? Did you see them in the water? Did they make it to shore?" So very few answers could be positive. It was a time of exceptional sadness for all of us.

Friendships formed while men are prisoners of war have the potential of lasting until the end of time. When this bonding ends through death in the prison setting, the survivor endures an excruciating period of mourning that is not like any other, even one involving a member of his own family. The sadness never seems to disappear; it goes on endlessly, leaving the bereaved one in a permanent state of mourning.

Occasionally, a new arrival joined us and great rejoicing followed by one or two of the men who knew him but sadly, after the first three days, new arrivals dwindled to zero and stayed there. All my inquiries received negative replies: Not one of my close friends survived. The eighty-one men with whom I was now associated were all strangers to me in our last prison camp.

The local Filipino people really earned our admiration and respect. We owe them so much. Many of the villagers donated chickens to feed us. They cooked them and brought them to us from the village, a walk of considerable distance. Others placed a net across a nearby stream, then went upstream and began to beat the surface of the water with sticks as they worked their way down to the net. They managed to catch quite a number of small fish which they cooked on the spot. A Filipina nurse walked over the hills from her distant village bringing a six-ounce bottle of disinfectant and some cotton swabs. She worked diligently with every man, cleaning up wounds, removing dried blood, making everyone feel more comfortable.

After five days at this site it became obvious that our group was not going to grow beyond its present number. We needed expert medical care for many of our men. Two of our members made the swim to shore with compound fractures of the lower leg. Two men were suffering broken ribs, and one had a broken jaw. Several men needed treatment for bullet wounds. Another had a deep, open gash on one thigh which was highly susceptible to infection. He was in considerable pain. We needed help, help that could not be provided at this location. Furthermore, the Filipinos should not be expected to feed us forever. We must leave here as soon as possible.

When we made the final tally, we learned that from our original group of 750 men, only 83 had reached shore alive. We were destined to lose one more of our survivor group in three days' time when one of his fractured ribs would puncture his lung. Without competent medical help, there was no way we could save him. This reduced the number in our survivor group to 82. Strangely, not one of our doctors, dentists, or medical corpsmen survived. Dr. Heidger, the doctor whom I credited with saving my life at Davao, was lost. Dr. Tremaine, a good-natured giant of a man who was held in high esteem by all POW s, was also lost. Chaplains Morris Day and Joseph La Fleur did not show up as survivors.

My good friend Edmon Massee from my home town of Glendale, California went down with the ship, thus ending our dreams of establishing the Lugao Amateur Radio Network across the United States. Ray Zelinsky, with whom I traded haircuts at Lasang, didn't survive. He and I had such good laughs together. I'll never forget him. Gene Shevlin, my classmate from flying school, offered to trade assignments with me when the Army Air Corps first sent us to the Philippines. He thought he was too tall to fit into the cockpit of a pursuit plane. Unfortunately for me his squadron commander was against the change. Gene failed to make it to shore. Jon, my bunkmate at Lasang, and Liz, whom I met on the ship, were men I had hoped to have as life-long friends but they, too, failed to show up as survivors. But strangest of all was the loss of the two men with whom I shared the granite rock. We were touching each other when the torpedoes struck the *Shinyo Maru*. I survived, they didn't. This continues to challenge my mind. I'll never understand how it could happen. It haunts me to this day.

Lt. Col. Otto Fischer, ranking member of our survivor group, acting together with Capt. John Morrett, approached the Filipinos about moving farther along the coast to Sindangan. The people of Liloy believed there was a Filipino doctor there who could provide us with medical help for our wounded. Some hinted that individuals there might be able to put us in touch with our own forces. This was indeed a plus. Sindangan was approximately 25 kilometers from Liloy, much too great a distance to carry the wounded on litters, so arrangements were made for three sailing vessels about 40 feet in length. We planned to leave at night and if the breeze held we would arrive before dawn.

That night, after it was dark, we trekked quietly from our bivouac down to the departure area. Some men walked, some rode on the backs of *carabao*, the Philippine water buffalo. Those who were seriously wounded were carried on travois behind *carabaos*. As soon as the first boat was loaded with most of the wounded, it set sail. The remainder of us, depending upon our arrival time, were quickly loaded and started on our way.

I climbed over the side of the last boat and settled in near the stern. These were working vessels, so there was really no formal arrangement of seating. We simply sat any place on the bottom of the boat where we thought we could be comfortable. There were many tatami mats in each boat. These mats, woven of rice straw, were available to each of us to smooth out some of the bumps and ruts beneath us. We didn't realize as we set sail how important those mats would become.

Carabao carrying wounded to beach: too sick to walk

The breeze that propelled our boat was not a brisk one by any means, and as daylight approached it gradually deserted us. There we sat, completely becalmed, within sight of our goal. It was a beautiful day on the Sulu Sea. Under normal conditions we might have considered ourselves lucky to be stranded in such an ideal setting. But under the present circumstances, we were feeling somewhat nervous and very vulnerable.

Suddenly, someone in the bow of our boat yelled, "Plane! Plane!"

My God! There it was! A Japanese patrol plane was flying directly toward our bow about 50 feet above the water. Talk about a panic—every man in the boat was frantically trying to pull a tatami mat over his body. Those of us who were pilots warned the men around us to be sure no parts of their bodies were visible outside the mat. A pilot can see very clearly from a low altitude.

"Everybody still. Don't move a muscle," came the final warning.

When the Japanese plane flew by us, the Filipino fisherman was seated, calmly relaxed, in the stern of the boat. His arm rested on the tiller, while he casually waved his free hand at the pilot. For all the pilot knew, the fisherman was returning with his morning catch protected from the hot Philippine sun by a layer of tatami mats. The pilot saw nothing suspicious so he continued on his flight until he disappeared into the distance. We breathed a sigh of relief but stayed covered until our Filipino helmsman felt it was safe for us to reappear.

We were not yet out of harm's way. We were still becalmed, but in a short while little flutters of the sail gave us hope that the breeze was rising. Then the sail began to fill and soon we were on our way again. When our native helmsman sighted the village of Sindangan, he headed our boat straight for the shore. When we reached shallow water he tied off the tiller, walked toward the mast and began to take in sail. One of our leaders ordered all who did not have broken eardrums to go overboard and wade in as fast as possible. The rest of us waited until the boat ran aground on the sand close to shore. Then we stepped over the side and waded quickly to the beach. The last man had barely cleared the sand and disappeared within the canopy of palm trees that ringed the shore when the Japanese patrol plane passed over our empty boat on its return flight. God was with us on that day.

The people of Sindangan were very good to us. They offered to take a number of our escapee group into their homes as guests so we could be sheltered and fed. Lt. Ralph Johnson and I were assigned to the same family, a guerrilla lieutenant, his wife and infant child. Those who were unassigned to a family stayed in a sheltered lean-to alongside one of the mountain trails to the west of the village.

The first meal with our foster family again reinforced our convictions about the graciousness of the Filipino people. Ralph and I were really hungry. We had eaten very little since the day of our escape. Consequently, we were looking forward to a good dinner with the Lieutenant and his young wife. As she placed the food before us, we greedily went to work on it and soon ate at least half our allotted portion. As we began to slow down and relish the taste of the food, we realized that a big part of our enjoyment was due to the fact that we were eating rice, not cracked corn. This awareness began to arouse my suspicions, so I looked over at the plates from which the Lieutenant and his wife were eating. I instantly put down my utensils and stopped eating. I caught Ralph's eye and nodded toward their plates. He, too, stopped eating. Our hosts were feeding us rice. They were eating cracked corn.

Ralph and I immediately told them that we would not continue eating unless both staples were mixed together so all of us were eating the same food. We further insisted that each of us eat cracked corn at our next meal, unless they really wished to consume their remaining store of rice. Our few remaining meals with them featured cracked corn. This episode again awakened us to the inherently kind nature of the Filipino people. They were willing to sacrifice their own health to improve ours. Ralph and I had a bit of adventure each day as we left and returned to our adopted home. A stream ran by the residence on its way to the ocean, cutting us off from the village. Since the rivers along the western coast were all at flood stage, we walked a considerable distance upstream. Then we removed what few articles of clothing we were wearing and placed them carefully into the crowns of our newly acquired woven hats. Then holding the hats at arms' length above our heads, we faced upriver, stepped into the water and quickly started a side-skipping movement across the river until we reached the other side, well below the place we had started. By the time we put our clothes back on our bodies were dry and we were on our way to the village.

On our last day in Sindangan, Ralph and I were on our way to the lean-to which was on the other side of the village. The sun disappeared behind a large dark cloud bank that stretched across the ocean. We could see rain falling on the ocean and the heavy clouds above us were churned in all directions by the wind. We heard the sound of planes somewhere above the overcast, and up in the clouds a single patch of clear sky momentarily opened up. As we watched this rapidly changing scene, a flight of three Japanese sea planes came spiraling down through the hole and prepared to land in the bay. They apparently wished to take cover near land, where they would be protected until the storm blew over.

In a matter of minutes, six or seven guerillas with carbine rifles took prone positions behind the various rocks and trees near the shore. We warned them that they should wait to fire until all three planes had landed and moved in near the shore. If one plane was able to take off again, it would bring others back to bomb the village. All of these men had possessed their carbines for some time, and they were really eager to fire them in an actual engagement. They had no love for the Japanese. Ralph and I wondered if we could possibly talk them into waiting. The first plane was nearing the shore, the second was not far behind, but the third was just landing when one of the Filipinos opened fire on the plane nearest the shore. This started a veritable barrage of fire from the other Filipinos. The Nip in the rear cockpit began to return fire and all planes moved back out into the farthest section of the bay. The Filipinos continued firing until the planes were out of range. As soon as the storm moved on, two of the planes took off carrying both crew members of the first plane. The plane was abandoned and left floating. Apparently the Filipinos had either wounded the pilot or disabled the plane.

At this point, Ralph and I told the Filipinos to go home as fast as possible and evacuate their families, and to warn all other families as well. We hurried up a small hill near the beach on our way to the other members of our group. Although the hill was relatively small, the climb to the top was a steep one. By the time we reached the summit we heard the planes returning, so we quickly concealed ourselves in some dense shrubbery. In moments three float planes swooped down over our hill so close we felt we could almost reach up and touch them. Then they continued their downward path over the village homes, dropping bombs as they went. As they reached the far side of the row of homes, they climbed up and flew on into the distance. I fervently hoped that none of the Filipinos or their family members were injured.

Neither Ralph nor I were able to assess the damage. The houses were surrounded by heavy growths of shrubs and tall trees and it is likely that the pilots simply dropped their bombs in a random pattern. Although I saw heavy puffs of smoke rising from the area, they appeared to be from the explosion of the bombs and not from fire; because the homes were so tightly grouped, it's hard to imagine they escaped without some damage. We hurried from the hill and continued on to our hillside bivouac area. After reporting the incident to our commanding officer, the decision was made to leave Sindangan and move north to Siari.

In the morning we left early and followed the trail to Siari. When we reached the beach in Sindangan, we found the Japanese plane had floated to shore, but we couldn't afford the time to go over it carefully to determine why it had not taken off.

Siari really surprised us. It was as close to being a living movie set as any area I had seen. It was located on the shore of a small lagoon ringed by exotic-looking palms. As we stood on the shore admiring this magnificent view, we could see that the shore to our right extended much farther into the ocean than the land on the left. When the sun began to set, the right side of the lagoon was lit from behind, throwing it into a beautiful silhouette. The trees reflected in the water of the lagoon and the sun struck the lagoon itself at a low angle making a big part of it shine like a mirror. It was indeed a very inspiring scene.

One of Siari's leading citizens very kindly allowed us to sleep on the living room floor of his beautiful home. On this particular evening, however, Colonel McGee indicated that he wanted all of us to follow him to the edge of the lagoon. He waited until the sun disappeared below the horizon, then he led us to the edge of the beach. We sat quietly on the sand along the line of the palm trees. Col. McGee sent men beyond the ends of our position to function as perimeter guards so we couldn't be surprised by a Japanese patrol.

Col. McGee was a remarkable man and an admirable soldier. He was a graduate of West Point, an outstanding infantry officer, and was destined to rise to the rank of General. He had little patience with men who did not perform in accordance with their rank. He expected near- perfection from himself and from the men who served under him. He was not with us at Lasang, but he was a prisoner with us at Davao Penal Colony.

He sailed with the remainder of the men at Davao when they left two months before us. The POWs on that ship were permitted to come out of the hold even at night to use the toilet facilities built over the edge of the ship's deck. While the ship was anchored in Zamboanga Harbor, the Colonel persuaded a few men on deck to engage in a minor argument and subsequent tussle to attract the guards' attention while he ran to the opposite side of the deck and dove overboard. Apparently the guards were unaware of his escape. He was swimming toward the shore when he saw a Filipino paddling his native canoe. He rapidly swam toward him and grabbed his boat. The Filipino had no idea what was happening to his craft until the Colonel pulled himself up out of the water and rolled in beside him. Of course he was very startled, but the Colonel's explanation of who he was and where he came from, calmed the native down and at the same time won him over as an ally. Col. McGee had served in Zamboanga prior to the war, so he knew the city and its neighborhoods quite well. He asked his boatman to let him off at a point with which both he and the native were familiar so he could make his way from there along the edge of the city and on into the mountains beyond. Eventually, with help from Filipinos he knew, he managed to reach a guerrilla outpost commanded by American personnel. The outpost was equipped with two-way radio, so word of the Colonel's arrival was transmitted to our forces. It was in this same way that word was sent to him about our group of escapees and he was ordered to Sindangan to assume command of our unit. We were happy with our own leadership but it was very reassuring to have a commander who knew so much about the area in which we now found ourselves.

The Colonel also discovered two radio operators among our own survivor group, and in no time had recruited the use of radio equipment from the Filipinos to put us in touch with the guerrilla outpost up in the mountains of Mindanao. The Colonel's assignment was the luckiest thing that could possibly have happened to us.

As we sat gazing out onto the waters of Siari Lagoon, we couldn't help but wonder why we were waiting, yet no one talked about it. It was as if to utter the word we were thinking about would put a hex on the whole operation. At about 9:00 p.m. the Colonel rose from his spot and waved us all back to the house.

The second evening of waiting there was still no mention of what we were waiting for. We pretty much followed the pattern of the first night, with the exception of one small incident. While sitting at the end of the row of waiting escapees again, I was startled to see a Filipino jauntily walking along the beach. If he continued on his present course he would pass directly in front of us. I wondered why he had not been stopped by our perimeter guard and turned back. When he was just a few yards from us, I felt compelled to challenge him because he was completely unaware of our presence and I didn't want him to know how many of us were waiting. So I spoke to him rather quietly.

"Hey, Joe. Where are you going?"

For a moment he came to a complete halt, searched in our direction with his eyes, and then seeming to find us in the darkness, he came over and squatted next to us. I asked him what he was doing here at this time of the evening. Then he said to me "Sir. I hab (have) just come to remoobe (remove) my bowels."

Then he smiled broadly and kindly accepted my suggestion that he look for a place to "remove" his bowels back in the area where he had come from.

The third evening we were aroused from our dreamy survey of the scene before us by the living image of the word we had been afraid to say. Across our line of vision came the long, low, dark shape of an American submarine. Talk about excitement! What do you do when you want to jump up and dance, and yell as loud as you can yell, and cavort around the beach like an absolute idiot to express the pure joy that is bursting within you, and you don't dare make a sound? Of course, a few moments of serious thought curbed my excitement even more when I recalled that submarines are not known for their overabundance of interior space. How many of us could they possibly take?

The submarine had stopped its forward motion now and four men from the sub manned a black rubber dinghy that was nearing our position. Every one in our survivor group had been assigned a priority number by our Filipino doctor, the number reflecting their relative physical condition, which would in turn determine their eligibility for a place on the submarine. My number was 23. I had been an ardent student of submarine movies for a long time, and I was positive I would not make the trip this time. I knew that at best, the first three or four men might make it, but not those of us who had the larger numbers. As a result I was with many others who were crowded around the seriously wounded men requesting, "Tell my parents I'll be home soon." "Let my wife know I'll probably be home on the next sub." "Get word to my girlfriend that…"

And so it continued until we became aware that Col. McGee had finished talking with the men from the sub, and they were paddling back.

As he walked from the water up the beach, we all gathered around him to hear the verdict. He hesitated for a moment, looking around to see that everyone was nearby, then he spoke.

"Men, I have just spoken with the Executive Officer of the sub and he said they would take all of us!"

I couldn't believe my ears. Eighty men, and they were going to take all of us, but how were we to get out to the sub? Almost before I uttered the question in my mind, Col. McGee spoke.

"All of you who are able to walk, hurry down to the water's edge and get in one of the small bancas waiting there and the owner will paddle you out to the sub. A crew member will help you get on the sub. Follow their directions from there on."

I turned toward the ocean and saw a miniature flotilla of a hundred or more native oarsmen paddling their small canoes as fast as they could across the lagoon. They came streaming out of the dark section of the extended side of the lagoon, appearing almost magically as they slipped through the end of the shadows. In a few moments they reached the shore in front of us. Some canoes were carrying bamboo poles which the Filipinos quickly assembled and bound together on the beach, creating rafts on the spot to transport our stretcher cases out to the submarine. The Filipinos are masterful workers of bamboo and can perform near-miracles of construction with it in moments. The organization of all these natives was astounding, and I'm sure must have been largely arranged ahead of time by Col. McGee. The whole operation seemed to start at one instant then pour out endlessly like lava from a volcano.

As soon as one of the canoes arrived in the area where I was waiting, I ran to it quickly and hurried forward to the bow. Instantly my Filipino oarsman shoved his boat forward to free it from the sand. Then he jumped in, grabbed the paddle, and we were on our way.

I began to feel such a wonderful sense of well-being as the cool night breeze pushed against my face, and I felt each strong stroke of my boatman's paddle driving me toward that instrument of freedom out there in the lagoon. It waited to start me on my way home again. This was the real thing now. Something good was happening and I was actually involved in it. I didn't have to wonder how this would affect the chance of my becoming free once again. Thanks to God, I was free—and I was coming home.

Chapter 11

The Long
Voyage Home

My Filipino oarsman paddled furiously to get me out to the submarine. As our little native canoe got closer, the sub began to look bigger and bigger. I couldn't figure out how I was going to get up on that large rounded side; no one could maintain his footing on such a sharply curving surface. I thought the water next to the sub would be as smooth as glass out in the lagoon, but apparently there was a strong current entering the bay and the sub had to keep its engines turning at a moderate speed to maintain position. Our outrigger was bobbing up and down like a cork.

Then, when we were only a couple of canoe lengths from the side of the sub I saw, dimly through the dark, a man on the deck. He was bare from the waist up. He looked like Arnold Schwarzenegger to me. He was a big, muscular, healthy-looking guy. He had tied a rope to the rail of the boat, and he was way out on this big bulbous side hanging on to the rope with one hand and reaching out with the other to get whoever came near him.

Since there were no other small boats near us, my oarsman steered our outrigger directly toward the waiting crewman. Just about the time we expected to collide with the side of the sub, a swell lifted us high on the water. The crewman grabbed me by my upper arm. In the same way a father would lift his child's teddy bear off the floor and put it on a chair, that's the way he put me on the sub.

I didn't realize how much we had deteriorated. I knew that at one time I weighed myself in prison camp on a rice scale and my weight was less than ninety pounds, but I didn't know how much less. Anyway, with only one arm he lifted me and brought me across to the deck beside him; then he aimed me toward the conning tower. He urged me to hurry, so I moved as fast as the darkness and the unfamiliar surfaces beneath my feet permitted.

Other crewmen told me to climb up the iron rungs on the side of the conning tower and in a few minutes I was descending through the hatch and down into the interior of the sub. As I stepped from the ladder to the floor of the room, I saw several men facing a collection of gauges, levers, and panels of small colored lights which glowed steadily or blinked rapidly on and off. I felt sure these men knew precisely what to do to start their vessel moving toward the open sea and were ready to put it in motion in less than an instant. As I stood there partly mesmerized, a large hand came to rest on my bare shoulder, and with the slightest pressure turned me half-right and guided me along a lengthy passageway to the forward torpedo room. They put half of us, about 41 men, in the forward torpedo room and the other 41 in the aft torpedo room.

The officers and crew couldn't wait to get out of the lagoon. We admired that lagoon for its idyllic beauty; they feared it for its dangers. They wanted to get out of there fast. They were in shallow water; the sub was terribly vulnerable. They didn't want to stay there an instant longer than they had to.

The cook stuck his bearded face through the entrance hatch to our room and told us that he knew of our circumstances and understood that we were probably very hungry, but until we were safely underway it would be impossible for him to prepare any food for us. He did promise us that as soon as he was allowed to return to his galley he would send in a cup of hot soup for every man—a promise that he soon kept. Just before he turned to leave us he said, "Tomorrow at breakfast we'll treat you right, believe me."

Our room appeared to be well-filled. It seemed to us that all our group must surely be aboard. Then we heard the painful cries of some of our seriously wounded. We had forgotten they would be the last to arrive because the natives had to complete their rafts before they could be transported to the sub.

WAR DEPARTMENT

THE ADJUTANT GENERAL'S OFFICE

WASHINGTON 25, D. C.

IN REPLY TO:

Q. Sneddon, Murray M.
I-N 298160

bar

26 October 1944

Mrs. Richard Sneddon
653 West Glenoaks Boulevard, Apartment 2
Glendale, California

Dear Mrs. Sneddon:

This will confirm my telegram of 25 October wherein you were informed that your son, Second Lieutenant Murray M. Sneddon, 0407072, has been returned to military control and is at present safe and recuperating in the Southwest Pacific Theater.

He was aboard a Japanese Army freighter transporting Americans who were prisoners of war of the Japanese Government from the Philippines when the freighter was destroyed. There were some survivors who made their way to a nearby shore, and fortunately, your son was among this group and I share with you the joy in the knowledge of his safety. I feel sure that if you have not already had a communication from your son that you will shortly enjoy the pleasure of a message direct from him.

While our telegram to you gave the APO number to which mail should be sent, I am again furnishing you with his address which is as follows:

Second Lieutenant Murray M. Sneddon, 0407072,
APO 923, c/o Postmaster,
San Francisco, California.

Knowing your desire to communicate promptly with your son the Chief of Staff has authorized that a cablegram of not to exceed twenty-five words be sent him at government expense. It is requested that in the event that you desire to send such a radiogram that it be dispatched by letter or telegram to the Casualty Branch, Adjutant General's Office, Room 3056, Munitions Building, Washington 25, D. C., from where it will be forwarded to your son.

May I assure you of my extreme pleasure in being able to transmit this information to you and please be assured that when additional information is received, it will be sent to you at once.

Sincerely yours,

Robert H. Dunlop

ROBERT H. DUNLOP
Brigadier General,
Acting The Adjutant General.

Letter confirming telegram, October 26, 1944

83 Yank prisoners rescued Oct 23/44
from Japs safe in Australia

GEN. MacARTHUR'S HEADQUARTERS, LEYTE, Oct. 23.—(UP)—The names of 83 American officers and men rescued from the Japanese several weeks ago after 2½ years imprisonment, and now safe in Australian hospitals, were announced today by Gen. Douglas MacArthur's headquarters.

The men are survivors of a Japanese transport sunk by an American submarine while prisoners were being transported north through the Philippines. Many other American prisoners were shot in the water and at least 50 were brutally executed, MacArthur had revealed earlier.

Two of the liberated Americans, First Lt. Richard L. Cook of Los Angeles and S/Sgt. Joseph T. Coles, Caso, Ala., elected to remain with the Filipino guerrillas who assisted them, MacArthur said.

All of the 83 men are in good condition except five recovering from bullet and grenade wounds, none of whom are listed as serious, it was announced.

The California men, all of whom will soon be returned to the United States, are: First Lt. Richard L. Cook, Los Angeles; First

Lt. James D. Donlon, 900 C st., Antioch; Second Lt. Murray M. Sniddon, 653 W. Glenoaks blvd., Glendale; Donald F. Gillen, 426 E. Palmer ave., Glendale; Sgt. Robert J. Kircher, Paradise; Corp. William T. Frederick, Ojai; Pfc. Omar A. Schoenborne, 339 Fourth ave., Redwood City; Pvt. Donald J. Grans, 5550 Huntington blvd., Fresno, and Pvt. Glen E. Kunkle, Long Beach.

WESTERN UNION

A. N. WILLIAMS
PRESIDENT

CLASS OF SERVICE	SYMBOLS
This is a full-rate Telegram or Cablegram unless its deferred character is indicated by a suitable symbol above or preceding the address.	DL=Day Letter NL=Night Letter LC=Deferred Cable NLT=Cable Night Letter Ship Radiogram

The filing time shown in the date line on telegrams and day letters is STANDARD TIME at point of origin. Time of receipt is STANDARD TIME at point of destination

WA789 66 GOVT=WASHINGTON DC 25 1152P

MRS RICHARD SNEDDON=

653 WEST GLENOAKS BLVD APARTMENT TWO GLENDALE CALIF=

THE SECRETARY OF WAR IS PLEASED TO INFORM YOU OF THE RECEIPT OF AN OFFICIAL REPORT IN THE WAR DEPARTMENT WHICH INDICATES THAT YOUR SON SECOND LIEUTENANT MURRAY M SNEDDON HAS BEEN RETURNED TO MILITARY CONTROL AND IS PRESENTLY RECUPERATING I THE SOUTHWEST PACIFIC AREA ADDRESS MAIL FOR HIM TO APO 923 C POSTMASTER SAN FRANCISCO CALIFORNIA UNTIL HE ADVISES YOU OF NEW ADDRESS LETTER FOLLOWS=

J A ULIO THE ADJUTANT GENERAL.

THE COMPANY WILL APPRECIATE SUGGESTIONS FROM ITS PATRONS CONCERNING ITS SERVICE

Report of rescue and confirming telegram

There are sloping tubes in both the forward deck and the aft deck which are normally used to load torpedoes into the two torpedo rooms. In emergencies, wounded men can be carefully drawn down through these sloped tubes into the interior of the sub with little or no pain, but in our need to leave as soon as possible there was no time for delicate handling. Men with compound fractures of the lower leg were held, as gently as possible, under the arms and lowered slowly from man to man straight down the conning tower. Despite the careful handling they received from the crew, they expressed their pain through cries and moans, as the weight of a foot pulled against the fracture. Their makeshift splints of tree branches were just not adequate for this type of handling.

Two or three cots were unfolded and set up on the floor of our room to accommodate men with fractures or deep wounds. We were told that any of us who wished to try the torpedo racks along both sides of the room could do so and crewmen would be happy to bring in some of their heavy winter clothing to soften the edges of the steel racks. I didn't like the thought of sleeping on the floor. I had endured a couple of years or more sleeping on flat boards. Sleeping up on the torpedo racks appealed to me and I found it quite comfortable, especially with the padding of heavy clothing underneath my body.

When I first realized I was going to board a submarine, I feared that I might not be able to live in such close conditions for a number of days. But when I actually arrived in the forward torpedo room I learned my fears were unnecessary. Air was constantly circulated around the entire boat by a series of fans. The feeling of fresh air against my face was very pleasant and made me feel as if I were outside enjoying a nice sea breeze.

The fear I'm really talking about here is claustrophobia, the fear of being confined in a small space. This fear I didn't experience. However, outside this cocoon-like space in which we were dwelling a war was being waged, and any threat to our boat frightened me a great deal. That fear was with me throughout our entire trip, especially during our transit of the Sibutu Passage.

Once we were underway, a single crewman was on watch in our torpedo room around the clock. During any emergency two men stood watch together to handle the firing of our four torpedoes, if needed. Since these men changed their watch about every four hours, we had several men to answer our questions about what had been happening in the world during our captivity. The poor guys endured a real barrage of questions during all daylight watches.

One of them lost credibility with us when he made the ridiculous assertion that our forces now had airplanes that flew without propellers. You have to understand that many of us were trained military pilots, others were in materiel squadrons, servicing or repairing aircraft of every description. We were not a bunch of dummies: when it came to aircraft, our combined experience put us in a class with the best. So we were quite certain that only a poorly informed navy man, or one unusually susceptible to wild rumors, could make such a foolish statement. Of course, we learned later that we really owed him an apology. It was such an incredible idea to us that we just couldn't find it possible to accept it.

We learned also that our ship was the submarine *Narwhal*, sister ship of the *Nautilus*, the largest submarine afloat. She had performed many rescues like ours. Her crew had carried important personnel in and out of the Philippines. They had placed bales of counterfeit Japanese currency with the Filipinos to devalue the Japanese peso. Because of her huge size, she was used to carry arms and ammunition to the Filipino guerrillas as well. She had performed some unusual and important tasks, and now she was carrying us on the first leg of our journey home.

Breakfast was the one meal I dreamed of having when we were returned to American control. I wanted something salty. We sweated so much while work-ing in the rice fields and on the airfield while prisoners, yet we were never given salt. So after a good night's sleep, I looked forward to breakfast, our first meal on the *Narwhal*.

Soon after we awoke, ten men at a time moved along the central passageway leading to the mess hall. This was necessary because the balance in a submarine is very delicate. So ten men were allowed to go toward the galley, after which the balance of the boat was adjusted. Then another ten men were sent in, and so on. Of course we had men coming in from the aft torpedo room as well, so quite a bit of adjusting was necessary.

When my turn arrived, I jumped down from the torpedo rack and eagerly headed for the mess hall. As I reached a point where I began to pick up the odor of food from the kitchen, my dreams of that first meal quickly disappeared. I never before realized that American food was so greasy and fat. I smelled that greasy smell and it just about turned my stomach upside down. I was able to get into the mess hall but my stay there was terribly unpleasant. All I ate was bread, which was freshly baked, and jam. I just couldn't bring myself to face the bacon and eggs, sausages, fried potatoes, and other items I had dreamed about eating for so long.

Commander Titus, skipper of the *Narwhal*, set his sub on a southwesterly course along the northwest side of the Sulu Archipelago. Then carefully, with the crew on full combat alert, he ran *Narwhal* through the nine-mile-wide Sibutu Passage at the northeast tip of Borneo. We passengers had been informed of what was happening, and just how serious a risk our commander was taking to reduce the time of our trip, so despite our high degree of nervousness we sat very quietly until the episode ended. When the Executive Officer announced that we had successfully completed our transit through the dangerous Sibutu Passage and that we were now on our way again, we breathed a deep sigh of relief. Yet I wondered how many more of these very tense experiences we must endure before arriving home.

The run was made at night, on the surface. Japanese radar stations operated on both sides of the strait. Fortunately for us, the Japs failed to pick up our image on their scopes, so we passed through without incident. With that maneuver out of the way, the Commander redirected *Narwhal*'s course and headed almost due east, over the top of the Celebese Islands group.

The day after we were picked up by the *Narwhal*, we were moving steadily along our Celebese course when the boat's klaxon horn suddenly erupted: "Ah-oooo-gah! Ah-oooo-gah!"

My God—it was loud enough to wake the dead.

Immediately following the klaxon, a voice came over the ship's speaker yelling "Dive! Dive!"

Then to finish the job of leaving us in a complete state of shock, a loud, rapidly repeating bell tone came flooding over the speaker: "Bong, bong, bong, bong, bong, bong, bong..."

Instantly the submarine was alive with activity. A second torpedo man entered our compartment, slammed the hatch door behind him, and spun a wheel on the face of the door which firmly closed off our compartment from the rest of the boat. Both men reported their presence on watch, then stood near the torpedo tubes listening to information and orders transmitted over their intercom equipment.

In a very few minutes we became aware that the attitude of our boat was changing rapidly. We were going down at a very steep angle. The cots holding the badly wounded men were beginning to slide down the floor toward the torpedo tubes. Could this really be the way a submarine behaves during a normal dive?

We looked at the two torpedo men, trying to pick up a clue from their faces, but they didn't appear to be frightened. Then a voice came over the ship's speaker asking that all personnel not standing a watch go aft, immediately! This did not seem to me to be a normal request. I had been somewhat afraid up to this point, but now I felt our lives might be in jeopardy and my fear grew intense. The members of the crew later told us that they were very much afraid, but they tried to keep it hidden from us so we wouldn't panic.

The entrance to our room was opened up and we began to exit, but we had to cling to any natural hand holds on the walls to keep moving. As I inched my way up the passage to the control room, I could see in the adjoining rooms, chairs, boxes, many items not secured to the walls of the rooms sliding toward *Narwhal*'s bow. When I reached the near side of the control room, I heard the dive officer talking to his crew of men. His voice was calm, relaxed, as if he were conducting a friendly practice session.

"Okay. Let's level this bubble over here. Now, turn your wheel slowly...careful now...not too fast. Good ! That's coming nicely. I think we've got her where we want her. Now, we coaxed her back to an even keel...let's get her back down on manual, too."

I can't remember seeing such an outstanding example of a man handling pressure under fire than the one I had just witnessed. That dive officer was truly inspiring.

There was no need for any of us to continue farther. The voice on the boat's speaker announced that all personnel not on watch could return to quarters. I turned and made my way back to our torpedo room, crawled up to my nest in the torpedo racks and went to sleep. It was a treat to feel the fear leaving and my body becoming more and more relaxed. I thanked God once again for seeing us through a life-threatening situation.

When the emergency was over and we were cruising on the surface once again, our torpedo man explained to us what had happened. A lookout on the bridge sighted a plane bearing down on our sub from approximately nine miles away. The bridge was instantly cleared and the emergency dive order was sounded. When the sub started under, her stern dive planes jammed in full dive position, so we were heading down at a very steep angle, a condition we already knew from experience.

First attempts to stop the dive were unsuccessful. Only when *Narwhal*'s electric motors were run in full reverse did she respond by popping to the surface like a cork. Of course it was probable, at that moment, that the plane was directly over us, so the crew bypassed the normal system and executed the dive order again using manual control. If the pilot of the plane had seen us he might have chosen to drop bombs or depth charges, but thank God this time we were spared that experience.

On our fourth day we had passed through the tip of the Halmaheras and were heading for our destination in Dutch New Guinea when a lookout on the bridge picked up a plume of smoke on the horizon directly in line with our course. Other crewmen on the bridge continued to monitor that smoke and within a couple of hours established the fact that it came from the stacks of a large ship, and she was definitely Japanese.

Commander Titus was authorized to fire on enemy shipping if it was unescorted. So he made a careful search of the horizon, but failed to detect any other vessels in the vicinity. Since all conditions were go, he ordered the number one torpedo made ready for firing. The torpedo man in our forward torpedo room set the gyros in the torpedo and assured the Commander that all was ready for firing.

Commander Titus ordered *Narwhal* down to periscope depth, then he slowly began his approach. When we were only 1,000 yards from the Japanese ship he ordered the periscope up for another reading. To his great disappointment he saw that the hull of the ship bore three very large red crosses. It was a Japanese hospital ship. We shared his disappointment; all elements had seemed so perfect for a successful attack.

After *Narwhal* had successfully been spirited away from the area, we surfaced and resumed our course for New Guinea. Although everyone in our boat assumed the episode of the Japanese hospital ship was over, we in the forward torpedo room learned we had some unfinished business to attend to.

The torpedo had been set to activate a certain distance beyond our boat; the course and other essential information had been programmed into its gyros. Now it was necessary to remove all that old information in order to ready the torpedo for new data when Commander Titus wanted to fire it again.

Our torpedo man asked all of us who were sleeping on the starboard torpedo rack to step down on the floor and to clear all winter clothing from the rack. Then he opened the door of the torpedo tube, fastened block and tackle to the rear of the torpedo, and began to slowly draw the torp—as the crew preferred to call it— out of the tube and onto the rack. As the torpedo glided out onto the rack, we saw that it was made of gleaming brass. I estimated its diameter to be at least two feet, or more. I thought it would never stop coming out of the tube; it continued to grow longer, and longer, and longer. When it was fully out of the tube, we learned from the torpedo man that it was all of 21 feet long. Believe me, in the confined space of our room it looked positively monstrous. It was not difficult to understand how two of those could completely tear apart a ship the size of the *Shinyo Maru* and send it plunging to the bottom of the sea.

I was very much aware that at that moment I was standing within a foot or two of a torpedo that was fully intact. Its explosive charge was in its belly. It was still programmed to explode. I hoped there was no way it could be detonated here in our compartment. Even if it fell off the rack and rolled across the room it would kill most of us without even exploding. The proximity of this deadly instrument alone was enough to frighten anyone half to death. Fortunately for us, the torpedo man had drained the gyros and had made the other adjustments required. He was now pulling the torp back into its tube. When he closed and dogged down the door to the tube, I began to breathe comfortably once again.

As we climbed up on the torpedo rack to sleep for the night, we realized this was our last night aboard the *Narwhal*. We could hardly classify our journey as a routine trip but I, for one, was really happy to have been aboard. Not only had we been safely carried through the very heart of Japanese occupied territories, but we had learned a great respect for the men who fought this war with submarines. They had treated us well and we were exceedingly grateful.

A year or so after we reached home, an article appeared in *The Saturday Evening Post* magazine titled "Twenty Thousand Headaches Under the Sea." It was the story of the *Narwhal*—which the crew referred to as the Old Girl—and contained an account of many of the strange and unique tasks they were assigned during the war. Prominent among these stories was their meeting with us, and the impressions we left with them:

"The poor guys we picked up were the most pitiful looking bunch you ever saw. They were wearing old, beat up Filipino straw hats and ragged G-strings made of flour and sugar sacking. They were barefooted, and some of them were still carrying the half coconut shells they had held out to be slopped full of watery rice on the Jap ship. A lot of them had eardrums that had been blasted open by the concussion of the torp.

"It was worth everything to see those 82 faces when they came on board. They wore the look a dog wears when he has been lost a long time and sees somebody he knows. When you took hold of them and helped them down or up, they didn't weigh nothing.

"Getting the wounded down the hatches was a heartbreaking business. At the slightest touch of swollen and sensitive flesh against metal, the helpless ones groaned pitifully, although they set their jaws to avoid such betrayals of weakness. Such bumpings were kept down to a minimum. No fragile, eggshell Sevres china was ever handled more carefully.

"Trying to allay the hunger of the survivors was almost as bad as the hunger itself. There were hotcakes and butter and beef and fruit juices for the emaciated men to eat, but the first morning at breakfast, when they had each wolfed down five or six hotcakes and between them had consumed 14 pounds of butter, their sick, long-empty stomachs rebelled, and many of them vomited what they had eaten."

The sickening smell of gangrene began to filter through the sub. It was, the Old Girl's crew said, a very hard smell to get used to. It turned your stomach over. But they tried not to let the 82 see how it affected them, and were careful to talk about it only when those in their care couldn't hear them.

Sketchily the crew managed to outfit their guests with shoes, caps and dungarees. But when the 82 made ready to disembark at an advanced base, they put their flour sack rags and their battered Filipino straw hats back on once more. It was as if they regarded those filthy garments as badges of honor and as symbols of the things they had endured. And no one of the sub blamed them for feeling that way about it."

Early in the morning of the fifth day of our journey, we docked at the tiny island of Woendi in Geelvink Bay, New Guinea. It was hard to say goodbye. I wanted to tell all the officers and men how much I loved them for bringing us here at such great risk to their own lives, but men are not supposed to talk in such terms to other men. So all I could do was shake each hand and, with eyes brimming with tears, say goodbye to the blurred faces before me. As I crossed the gangplank to shore I could see *Narwhal*'s crew already preparing to get under way again and I was sure someone needed their help as we had.

"Bon voyage, *Narwhal*; we thank you beyond the power of words to express for starting us safely on our long voyage home. May God's presence go with you always, on the surface or submerged."

As I turned my attention to the dock, I noticed that a small group of men had gathered to see what was going on. Perhaps they had been notified that a submarine was due to arrive this morning. When they saw us, I'm sure they must have wondered what strange planet we had moved in from. I was a little curious about them, too, and about this small island they were living on.

I recognized a group of three Lockheed Catalina flying boats, all painted black, and four or five PT boats. Since the Catalina flying boats were generally used for long-range reconnaissance over water, and the PT boats were excellent for attacking in areas where ships could not maneuver well, like the clusters of islands we had all around us, it was not difficult to assume we must be on a small Navy installation.

It wasn't long before a member of the Navy approached us and suggested that we use their outdoor shower facilities first, and by the time we were finished they would have new khaki outfits waiting for us, including stockings and shoes. Following that, the mess hall would be ready to serve lunch.

We couldn't believe it. This was luxury first class. Just like walking into a store with an open purchase order. We couldn't get our old prison camp clothing off fast enough. As we dashed for a shower that was unoccupied, the cries of discovery began:

"Hey, look! Real soap! Boy, I never thought we'd ever see that again."

"Get a look at that water! Wow, it's so clean you can even drink it...no mud."

"Look what's coming now! Clean towels! Does anybody remember what those are for?"

"This is too much. I think I've died and gone to heaven."

It was such a treat to wash our scalps with soap and water, then briskly towel them off. I can't remember a time when I felt so clean and comfortable. The brand-new clothing was the icing on the cake. I felt so supremely happy I was ready to head for home right now.

My new shoes created a bit of a problem. I was still suffering from wet beri-beri. My feet and lower legs were quite swollen, so I couldn't wear my new shoes. I was given a pair of oversized hospital slippers to wear temporarily until the edema in my feet disappeared. I tied the laces of the shoes together and carried them with me wherever I went.

The Red Cross gave me my last pair of new shoes while we were at Davao. Those shoes went down with the *Shinyo Maru* to the bottom of the Sulu Sea. I was never permitted to wear them even once, but I had to carry them with me whenever I was sent from one camp to another. This pair was not going to get out of my sight. I vowed I would wear them before I got home.

I didn't want to leave my discarded clothing for someone else to handle, so I picked up my Japanese G-string, which I had stopped wearing some time ago. I had wound it like a turban around my head to soak up all the blood and discharge from my ears. When the discharge dried, the cloth became stiff and foul-smelling, so I happily dropped it in the nearest trash container.

The same fate befell my cut-off Filipino jeans. They were so badly torn during the torpedoing that they could barely hang on to my body. My Filipino straw hat was ancient when I first got it from a friendly native in Sindangan. I thought of taking it home as a keepsake, but I didn't think the members of my family would be willing to tolerate it for long on the wall of a clean house.

Lunch was being served as I entered the mess hall, so I grabbed a plate and began to walk down the line of steam tables. The food looked very appetizing, but again the smell of fried food switched my appetite off instantly. I found a few items which I thought I might be able to keep down, then left the mess hall and moved out into the fresh air once again. When all our group finished eating we were directed to the area where the PT boats were tied up. Col. McGee divided us into three smaller groups and each third boarded a different boat. We felt concern for the seriously wounded; they lay on their litters unable to move, but fully exposed to the view of planes overhead. Yet we felt happy for them because they were being transported more rapidly now. They had endured a lot of pain and deserved to receive the treatment they had needed right from the beginning. Within a few days we were due to arrive in Australia and their long suffering would be over. Soon we were shouting our thanks and goodbyes to the naval personnel standing on shore, then our PT boats raced across the waters while all of us watched warily for enemy planes. The Japanese island of Biak lay directly ahead: danger might arise there. Although the danger of our being discovered was very real, the distance to our objective was quite short. It really didn't take long for us to reach the island of Owi.

Owi was really nothing more than an airstrip that ran from one end of the island to the other. Military Engineers, or perhaps Sea Bees, made high-walled revetments on both sides of the runway to protect the planes. Most of the aircraft I saw in the revetments were unfamiliar to me, manufactured perhaps within the last two or three years.

When our PT boats approached Owi, their crews discovered they were unable to get us close enough to the shore so we could disembark without wading through the water. Soon an all-metal, flat-bottomed landing craft pulled in along side us and we scrambled over its high sides and down into its bare interior.

In only a moment or two we made contact with the shore, and the front wall of our boat came crashing down on the sand. Of course we didn't expect such an abrupt and noisy end to our short trip in the landing craft. It gave us quite a scare. For a moment we remained rooted to our position, fearing some new, unexpected activity might follow. When nothing more occurred, we prepared to move out onto the sand.

She really came as a complete surprise to us. There she stood, not more than 25 or 30 feet up the beach, directly in front of our landing craft. She was dressed in dark clothing, perhaps a WAVE dress uniform, and she was wearing lipstick. At first it seemed to me that was all I could see of her, that glowing red mouth. Of one thing I felt sure: she was an American girl.

As we faced this challenge before us, no orders were given to tell us how to proceed. So without hesitation or directions our group seemed to melt together like a confused, milling swarm of individuals, then just as quickly reformed itself into two clearly defined single lines. One passed to the left of her, the other to the right. No one approached her closer than ten feet; no one spoke to her. I felt truly embarrassed by the whole episode, yet I didn't have the courage to speak to her either. I suppose the most honest explanation any of us could make would be to say that the experience represented a natural reaction on our part when we saw our first young American woman in three years.

I have thought about that experience many times since it happened. I have remembered certain things that I was not conscious of at the time, yet mostly I have only added to my growing list of questions. There must have been some significance in her dress; no one wears a heavy dress uniform on assignment in a hot, tropical area.

She was on an air base where many servicemen and women are assigned, or pick up, rides to Australia or the United States. Perhaps she was waiting to return home, as we were, and was simply trying to fill the time until her flight left.

If she was returning home to the States, she would arrive in winter where her dress uniform would be quite appropriate, but why did she station herself so close to the front of our landing craft? Did she not know the size of our group, or had she, in some way, discovered that we were escaped prisoners of the Japanese returning home after a number of years of captivity? She may have decided that the only way she could see the effects of our imprisonment might be to locate herself as close as possible. I'm afraid I'll never know the answers to these questions.

We didn't stay long in Owi. Each of our three groups was ushered into a small passenger plane and a nurse was assigned to each group. We then took off immediately. Our nurse visited with each one of us during the flight to determine if there was anything she could do to alleviate pain or to help make us more comfortable. She asked about my feet because she noticed I wore those oversized hospital slippers. I told her about the beri-beri but assured her there was nothing anyone could do to remedy the problem. It was not a problem for medicines to solve; it was a nutritional problem that would disappear as I ate good food containing lots of vitamin B. I told her that I was mainly concerned with my ears, that both drums had been broken and had bled and drained for several weeks now. She suggested that if I experienced any pain during the flight to notify her and she would provide some form of treatment for me.

Not long after our takeoff, the pilot called our attention to an area below where we saw hundreds of ships of all sizes. The town we could see was Hollandia, and the ships made up a part of the vast armada that General MacArthur was assembling for his invasion force that would retake the Philippine Islands. When he left he told the Filipino people, "I shall return," and it certainly looked like he was going to keep his promise. We learned later that just eighteen days after our departure from the Philippines, MacArthur's forces landed at Leyte.

Our planes ended their first day's flight at Wewak in Australian New Guinea. Accommodation for the night were prepared for us in advance at the only place in Wewak where a group our size could be cared for, the base hospital. This resulted in an interesting and somewhat surprising experience for all of us.

One of the patients in our ward became curious about our group because so many of us entered together. He thought perhaps we had been in a recent battle in one of the coastal cities of New Guinea. When we informed him we were former prisoners of war from the Philippines, he wanted to know where the Japanese had imprisoned us. When we told him we were interned in the Davao area of Mindanao, his interest really began to perk up.

He had served as a bombardier on an American B-24 bomber. Approximately 30 days prior to our meeting at Wewak he was on a bombing raid over southern Mindanao. The target on which he dropped his last bombs before heading back to Wewak lay a few miles northeast of Davao City. He described it as an airfield under construction. We immediately responded enthusiastically, "That's it! That's the airfield we were working on!"

Then he mentioned that as he approached the field he saw through his bomb sight a group of lighted buildings. They were just a short distance from the beginning of the runway, and he assumed they may have housed Japanese Air Force personnel.

"No, no," we chorused. "That was us. That was our camp!"

Instantly his eyes no longer focused on us, and it was obvious his mind had returned to the thoughts that passed through his mind as he focused on the remembered image before him in his bomb sight. Then his voice lowered to almost a hushed whisper as he repeated, over and over again, "Oh, my God…Oh, my God…Oh, my G—"

Then, and only then, did we fully realize just how close we had come to being the target for his final bomb run that evening.

The next morning we resumed our trip and flew to Nadzab in Australian New Guinea. After an overnight stay we headed over Papua and the Coral Sea. While flying to Townsville on the coast of Australia, we crossed the Great Barrier Reef that runs along the northeast coast of Australia. The view of that great reef disappearing into infinity, both to the north and to the south beneath our plane, was a magnificent sight. From Townsville we headed due south to Brisbane, the mid-trip stopover on our long voyage home.

There we were put in the 42nd General Hospital. We were quarantined for ten days to get rid of a lot of the diseases we had. At the end of that time they gave us a chance to see some of the city of Brisbane. Six days later, it was time to go home. That's what I was waiting for, but they put us on a ship, of all things. It took us fourteen days on that ship to go all the way home. To make matters worse, when we crossed the International Date Line we had to endure Friday for a second time. Like Job, I felt as if I were being especially tested before I would be allowed to see my loved ones again. The military assigned me to a cabin with five other men, but I fooled them. I never spent a moment in that room. I slept on the top deck. If that ship was going to be torpedoed, no way was I going to have any difficulty getting off.

I'll never forget the day we arrived at the coast of San Francisco. It was a cold, windy winter's day in November. The whitecaps were kicking up all over the place. It was drizzling rain. The clouds were right down on the land. For all intents and purposes it was an absolutely miserable day, but not to me. We sailed underneath that Golden Gate Bridge and as we got to the other side of it I said to myself, "At last I'm home."

We docked very quickly. Our commandant called us together and gave us a little advance pay. He said, "Okay, you are on your own. As soon as the gangway is down, you can leave. I want you to report to the Presidio at Monterey, for sure, three days from now." So he let us go and then it was that I knew I had a problem. Even though I had desperately wanted to get home, I hadn't had any word from my parents in almost three years and I didn't know if they were still all right. I was terrified that one of my parents might have died during all this time and, frankly, I didn't think I could cope with that.

So, as I wandered down the street, heading towards downtown San Francisco from the docks, I was trying to think of what to do so I could get word about my parents before I tried to get in touch with them. I made a couple of attempts but they didn't work. Then I remembered something that I'm surprised I even thought of.

I had an aunt and uncle someplace in the San Francisco area whom I had not seen since I was a child. They had a very peculiar vocation. My uncle was a casket maker and my aunt did all the beautiful sewing of the satin linings and things on the interior. I thought to myself, "I shouldn't have any trouble locating them." So as soon as I came to a drug store, I ducked inside. I got a handful of nickels and went into the phone booth, got out the yellow pages, and looked up casket makers. Sure enough, there were several. So I called up the first one and I asked if they had anybody by my aunt and uncle's name working there, and they said, "No, we're sorry, nobody by that name works here." But then I tried more and eventually I got one where the person answering said, "Just a minute," and I knew I had hit pay dirt.

My uncle came to the phone and when I told him who it was, he nearly exploded with excitement. He said, "Where are you?" I answered, "Hang on, I'll find out." So I walked out of the phone booth, went outside in the rain, and looked at the street signs on the corner and came back and told him where I was. He said, "Stay there, don't move. We'll be right down to get you." So I waited a few moments and then ventured back outside again. I stood under an awning to protect myself from the rain. It wasn't long before a slow-moving vehicle came creeping around the corner. I figured, "It's gotta be them." So I started to run out and suddenly the door was flung wide open and I leaped inside and, sure enough, it was my aunt and uncle.

All the way up to their home, all my uncle could say was, "You've just got to call your folks. You've just got to call." He assured me they were just fine. They had been out of the country, up in Canada for a while. My father was working up in Alaska, but they had returned. My aunt said my little sister had really changed. When we got to their home she showed me a picture of her they had received recently. When I left she was just a freckle-faced kid, and here now was this beautiful young teenager who just looked like a little movie starlet to me. In the meantime, my uncle had been putting through the call with the operator and I was expecting that he would tell my folks that I was there and that I would get to talk to them then. Instead, as soon as the operator began to ring the house he shoved the receiver in my hand.

I was terrified. What do you do in a case like that? When the person answers, do you say, "Hi, it's me" and have one of them drop dead on the floor? I figured I had to do something to delay so when my father answered the phone I said, "Mr. Sneddon?" He answered, "Yes." I continued, "Mr. Sneddon, I'm calling on behalf of the Armed Services. I was wondering if you might have a place at your Thanksgiving table this year for a serviceman away from home." He thought a moment then replied, "Well, yes. I think we can do that." So, flush with this initial success, I rambled some more only to realize that he wasn't answering me, he was just listening. So I stopped talking. There was a momentary silence, then he asked, "Is this Murray?" And I confessed, "Yes, it is, Dad."

Well, he burst into tears. He really was sobbing. He couldn't say another word. My mother, who had been standing nearby, was crying just as hard as he was but she could talk through it all. So I reassured them I was okay. Everything was fine, but it was mandatory that I stay up there two more days. I had to report to Monterey. My mother said, "Don't worry. We are going to come up to San Francisco tonight. We'll come on the train. I'm sure we can get permission." I asked, "Do you think you could get Fee to come, too?" My mother said, well, she thought she could. I thought, "Now that's a good sign. Surely my mother isn't going to bring a married woman up to welcome her son home from the war."

So the next morning my aunt and uncle and I were down at the station bright and early. We hardly got there when we saw a slow-moving train gliding in on the track that was designated for their arrival. But when I looked at it, I was really puzzled. There was nobody in it. I could see nobody at the windows, nobody. It looked like a ghost train of some kind. It moving ahead slowly and finally stopped—still no activity. I began to get nervous. I thought, well maybe this is one they are just preparing to load and it will go out and theirs will come in later. But about that time from one car in advance of me came a conductor down out of the car. He put his little stool down below the bottom step and he moved to one side. Through that open door came a blur. It was Fee. She ran towards me like an Olympic sprinter. She never stopped until she hit my open arms. Running right behind her was my mother and some distance back my father, forever the gentleman, brought up the rear. Then in what seemed like an instant, I had in my embrace the three people whose love had brought me home. It was the high of all highs of my life. I've never known another experience which for sheer depth of emotion could match it.

We went in the car up to my aunt and uncle's house and all the time, questions, questions, my parents wanting to know if I was really okay. But after a while the questions tapered off and my aunt and uncle and my folks got involved together. This was the moment I was waiting for. I got a hold of Fee and led her away to a quiet place. I told her how much I had thought about her and how much I wanted her to marry me. To my great joy, she said she would. We were married in less than a month. Marrying Fee was the most brilliant thing I've ever done in my life. She is my life. Without her I am simply half a person. I love her so dearly.

I lost both my parents in 1984. They died within six months of each other, but not before I entered their room one day and quietly shut the door behind me. I sat down in front of them. I took their hands in mine. I looked into their faces and told them how much I loved them. I told them how much I appreciated the values they had instilled in me as a youth. And I thanked them for always taking me to Sunday School and church from the time I was just a little baby, because it was what I learned in church that gave me the endurance that allowed me to keep going until my chance for freedom arrived.

I think you can understand, having read my story, that I came home with a lifetime supply of unpleasant memories. Yet those three highlight experiences; my survival and escape from the torpedoed ship, my marvelous homecoming, and my marriage to Fee were of such magnitude that they just seemed to throw the balance of all my experiences over onto the positive side. So despite the occasional nightmares I still have after all this time, and despite the times I wake up crying in the middle of the night, and despite the persistent memories of starvation and disease—and all the killing and the dying and death—I know, way down deep in my soul, that I am without a doubt one of the most blessed men on the face of this earth. For that inestimable gift, I sincerely thank God.

DEATH MARCH SURVIVOR HERE

"When the torpedoes hit 750 of us American prisoners were down in the hold of the prison ship. The brown devils threw grenades into the hold when the ship started breaking up and some of us lucky ones found ourselves swimming in the ocean."

This graphic description of one of the war's most atrocious incidents was revealed yesterday by First Lieutenant Murray M. Sneddon, survivor of the infamous "March of Death," when he was naturalized as an American citizen before Federal Judge J. F. T. O'Connor.

ON PRISON TRANSPORT

Lieutenant Sneddon was on board a Japanese prison transport headed for Japan after the surrender of Bataan when two torpedoes from an American submarine struck the ship.

"Of the 750 of us who had outlasted that terrible march only 83 survived — and I was one of the lucky ones," Lieutenant Sneddon said.

He described how scores of his "buddies" had drowned before his eyes when the group started the two-and-one-half-mile swim to the Mindanao shore.

"I would have swum it even if it had been 500 miles, after what I went through in that prison camp for 30 months and in that battened-down hold in that hell ship," Lieutenant Sneddon said.

After living with guerrillas and later being taken to Dutch New Guinea in an American submarine, Lieutenant Sneddon was in a hospital for 33 days, with both eardrums blown out.

He was married recently to his Glendale sweetheart.

BATAAN HERO—Lieutenant Murray Sneddon, survivor of Bataan death march and torpedoing of Jap prison ship, with his bride as he was naturalized in Federal Court here yesterday.
—Los Angeles Examiner photo.

Glendale Hero Who Fled Jap Ship Marries

Ending an engagement which was prolonged because the prospective bridegroom was in a Japanese prison camp, Lt. Murray Sneddon, Glendale war hero, and Miss Fiona Mountain, also of Glendale, were married at the First Presbyterian Church there yesterday.

Lt. Sneddon recently returned to the United States after escaping from a Japanese prison ship when it was torpedoed by a U.S submarine. He had been a prisoner since Corregidor. During the two and one-half years, Lt. Sneddon was in the camp, his fiancee received only one postcard from him.

'DEATH MARCH' SURVIVOR WEDS

Lieutenant Murray Sneddon, Army Air Force pilot who went through the horrors of the infamous death march to Camp O'Donnell following the fall of Bataan, was married yesterday to his childhood sweetheart, Miss Fiona Mountain, in the Glendale Presbyterian Church.

The ceremony, attended by a few close friends, was performed by the Rev. Dr. David Calderwood in the church chapel. Faye Mountain, sister of the bride, acted as bridesmaid and Harris Shanalin was best man.

Following the ceremony the couple left on a ten-day honeymoon.

Dec. 8 1944

MARRIED—Lieut. Murray Sneddon, survivor of the Bataan "Death March," with his bride and childhood sweetheart, Fiona Mountain. They were married in Glendale Presbyterian Church yesterday and left on a 10-day honeymoon.
—Los Angeles Examiner photo.

News reports of Murray & Fee's Wedding

Usually my mother spent most of the day listening to the radio, hoping to hear news of the Philippines. On the day that the news of my escape and rescue was announced, she was attending a church circle meeting. On returning home, she could hear the phone ringing inside. Upon answering she was informed by a friend that she had heard a news broadcast detailing the escape of a group of war prisoners and she was reasonably certain that she had heard my name mentioned among those rescued.

The phone continued to ring with similar stories coming from other friends and relatives. My mother kept a record of these calls. As you can see, a total of 82 people called to inform her of the good news.

Phone calls received from relatives and friends upon hearing radio broadcast

"Information Copy"

QUALIFIED FOR OVERSEAS DUTY

PHYSICAL EXAMINATION FOR FLYING

(See AR 40-100, 40-105, 40-110)

A TRUE COPY
RCWeismann

R E WEISMANN, Maj, MC

1. SHELDON, Murray McIvor, 1st Lt., AC O-407072 25 4
    (Last name) (First name) (Middle initial) (Grade and arm or service) (Serial No.) (Age) (Years service)

2. AAFRS#3, Santa Monica, Calif. Returned from Overseas, Oct 41, Qualified
    (Address) (Purpose of examination) (Date and result last examination)

    Pilot .... Flying time as: Pilot None ..; observer - ..; pilot None ..; observer - ..
    (Aeronautical ratings) (Total) (Total) (Last 6 mos.) (Last 6 mos.)

3. Temperature .98.6.. Vaccinations: Typhoid series, No. III .. Last 1940 ..; smallpox 1941 ..; reaction Immune
    (Date)

4. Medical history.
    (In the case of applicant include family. Has he ever had epilepsy, enuresis, headaches, dizziness, vertigo, fainting, stammering, tic, somnambulism, pavor nocturnus, migraine, insomnia, phobias, anxiety trends, irritability, apathy, elation, depression, sensory disturbances, amnesia, spasms, unconsciousness, repeated episodes of alcoholism, encephalitis, pneumonia, syphilis, renal calculi, tuberculosis, asthma, hay fever, repeated colds, mastoiditis, sinusitis, tonsillitis, arthritis in any form, malaria, severe injuries, major operations, or other pertinent history? Explain fully.)

    1941-44: Dengue fever, 5 recurrences; no seq. 1942-43: Malaria; approxi-
    mately 40 recurrences; no seq. 1942-44: Amoebic Dysentery; no seq.
    1942-44: Deficiency diseases (beri-beri, scurvy, pellagra, jaundice); also
    scabies, tropical ulcers, venous thrombosis, bilateral, on occasions.
    7 Sep 44: Perforation of ear drum, bilateral; no treatment. All of fore-
    going occurred while Ex. POW, 27 Dec 1944: Hookworm; hosp (Contd Par. 37)

5. Eye: Inspection ..normal..   Nystagmus ..none..
6. Associated parallel movements ..normal.. Pupils: Equality ..equal.. Reaction ..normal..
7. Visual acuity: R. E., 20/ ..20.. correctible to 20/ .-. L. E., 20/ ..20.. correctible to 20/ .-.
8. Depth perception (uncorrected) ..15.. mm. With correction .-. mm.
9. Heterophoria at 6 meters: Eso ..0.. Exo ..1.. R.H. ..0.. L.H. ..0.. Prism divergence ..7..
10. Red lens test .-. Angle convergence: PcB ..70.. mm. Pd ..64.. mm. .-.
11. Accommodation: R. ..8.. D. L. ..8.5.. D. Addition required for 50 cm. R. .-. L. .-.
    (Jaeger type): Right J. ..1-50.. correctible to J. .-. Left J. ..1-50.., correctible to J. .-.
12. Color vision ..normal..
13. Field of vision (form): R. ..normal.. L. ..normal.. Ophthalmoscopic: R. ..normal.. L. ..normal..
14. Refraction: R. reads 20/20 with .- S. ..○.. CAx .-° L. reads 20/20 with .- S. ..○.. CAx .-°
15. Ear: History of ear trouble ....(See Par. 4)...
16. External ear: R. ..normal.. L. ..normal.. Membrana tympani: R. ..normal.. L. ..normal..
17. Hearing (whisper): R. ..20../20. L. ..20../20. Audimeter (percent loss): R. .-. L. .-.
18. Nares ..normal.. Tonsils ..enucleated..
19. Teeth:
    (a)   Right   (Examiner's)   Left
       8 7 6 5 4 3 2 1   1 2 3 4 5 6 7 8
       16 15 14 13 12 11 10 9   9 10 11 12 13 14 15 16

       Indicate: Restorable carious teeth by ○; nonrestorable carious teeth by /; missing natural teeth by X.

    (b) Remarks, including other defects ....none....
    (c) Prosthetic appliances ....none.... (d) Classification ..II..
20. History of swing, train, air, or sea sickness ..denies..
21. Barany chair (when indicated with results) ..not done..
22. Posture ..good.. Figure ..slender.. Frame ..light..
    (Excellent, good, fair, bad) (Slender, medium, stocky, obese) (Light, medium, heavy)
23. Height ..68.. inches, Weight ..130.. pounds. Chest: Inspiration ..36.. Expiration ..33.. Rest ..34.. Abdomen ..26..
24. Skin and lymphatics ..Mastoidectomy scar, left.. Endocrine system ..normal..
25. Bones, joints, muscles ..normal.. /NH, NSND, slight atabrine discoloration, ND..
    Feet ..normal..
26. Heart ..normal..
27. Pulse rate ..78-84.. B.P.: S ..125-132.. D. ..74-78.. Schneider .-. Pulse immediately after exercise ..108..
    Two minutes after exercise ..86.. Character ..normal..
28. Arteries ..normal.. ; Varicose veins ..none..

    ¹ Semiannual appointment or cadet, commission in the Air Corps, commission in Air Corps Reserve, transfer to the Air Corps, or any other special purpose.
    ² I, II, III, or IV; see par. 3, AR 40-110.

    W. D., A. G. O. Form No. 64
    (May 10, 1941)

Physical exam and medical history, December 27, 1944

WAR DEPARTMENT
The Adjutant General's Office
Washington, D.C.

February 19, 1945

Mrs. Raymond P. Zelinsky
1820 Palmcroft Way, Northwest
Phoenix, Arizona

Dear Mrs. Zelinsky:

The War Department has now received the official list of prisoners of war on the Japanese freighter, which you were previously informed was sunk on September 7, 1944. It is with deep regret that I must now inform you that your husband is among those listed as lost when that sinking occurred. The War Department regrets its inability to entertain a probability of his survival and must now consider him to have died in action September 7, 1944. The date of receipt of this final evidence was February 14, 1945, the date upon which his pay will terminate and his accounts be closed.

The information available to the War Department is that the vessel sailed from Davao, Mindanao, August 20, 1944 with 750 prisoners of war aboard. The vessel was sunk by torpedoes on September 7, 1944, off the western shores of Mindanao. The indications are that relatively few of the prisoners had opportunity to leave the sinking ship and of those who did many were killed by enemy gun fire. A small number managed to reach shore and a close watch for others was kept for several days. The Japanese Government reports all of the prisoners as lost, indicating that no survivors are in the hands of that Government. There is no information as to what happened to the individual prisoners but known circumstances lead to the regrettable conclusion that all of the unaccounted for prisoners lost their lives at the time of the sinking.

It is with deep regret that I must notify you of this unhappy culmination of the long period of anxiety and suffering you have experienced. You have my heartfelt sympathy.

Sincerely yours,

J. A. ULIO
Major General
The Adjutant General

Letter to Mrs. Zelinsky, February 19, 1945

Two Years of Hell in Jap Prisons Told

Nov 27 1944

There is a long, horrifying story to tell about the experiences of 1st Lt. Murray Sneddon and still—in his words—there is little to say.

He has been to hell and he got back! In two and a half years in Japanese prison camps, he has endured and suffered beyond the realm of imagination.

The slight, soft-spoken officer wants to forget, but yesterday he told his story as he sat beside his mother, Mrs. Richard Sneddon, in their Glendale home, 663 Glenoaks Blvd.

It began when Bataan was surrendered to the Japs on April 9, 1942. Sneddon was stationed at Cabcaben Field, Bataan, with the 2nd Air Force Observation Squadron.

Death March Endured

He fell in line for the death march from Bataan—105 miles and nine days—to Camp O'Donnell. He had no food and little water. He saw men clubbed to death, shot and buried alive. He wanted to die but his spirit kept him alive and he made it to Camp O'Donnell.

Life became hopeless and hours dragged into days and melted away in weeks. Eighteen hundred men died in two months and the desire to live dwindled until only the thought of death filled the mind of every prisoner.

From there he was consecutively interned at three different camps, Cabanatuan, Bilibid Prison in Manila and Davao Penal Colony, where he was on a labor gang until March of this year.

During this time, the Air Force officer contracted malaria, beri beri, jaundice, tropical ulcers, scurvy, dysentery and numerous other ailments. He dropped from a normal 140 pounds to 90.

Prison Ship Torpedoed

The first hope of rescue came in August when the Yanks bombed a Davao airfield where he had been working repairing Japanese planes. Then on Aug. 20 he was loaded, along with about 750 other men, aboard a transport and put to sea.

Until Sept. 7, when a U.S. submarine torpedoed the Jap craft, all was darkness deep in the hold of the scurvy enemy transport. The men huddled together, sick and exhausted, not knowing or caring where they headed. They hoped for a miracle of escape and for some it came. They were in the Zamboanga

Gulf off Mindanao when the blast came. The ship reeled under the impact of two well-aimed torpedoes. It was every man for himself and Lt. Sneddon, along with 82 other survivors, made it. Swimming two and a half miles to shore, the weary Yanks were sheltered and treated by friendly natives until a submarine picked

LT. MURRAY M. SNEDDON, home after two and one-half years in Jap prison.

Jap Prison Horror Told

After two and one-half years in Jap prison camps, Lt. Murray M. Sneddon, son of Mr. and Mrs. Richard Sneddon, 653 West Glenoaks, has returned home.

Memories of the death march from Bataan, of hard labor and illnesses which cut his weight from 140 pounds to 90 pounds, of cruelty and deprivation which almost erased the desire to live—all these are happily growing a bit dimmer day by day.

Ship Torpedoed

Lt. Sneddon, an air force officer, was consecutively interned in four prison camps, Camp O'Donnell, Cabanatuan, Bilibid and Davao. In August he was one of 750 prisoners placed aboard a Jap transport and sent to sea. Destination not known. Nearly three weeks later a United States submarine torpedoed the ship. Sneddon and 82 others made it to shore. They were in Mindanao where friendly natives cared for them.

He remained on Mindanao until a submarine picked him up with others and took them to Dutch New Guinea, from where they were sent to Australia for hospital care and from there to the United States.

Sunday, at the First Presbyterian church, Sneddon will wed Miss Fiona Mountain, 22, to whom he has been engaged four years.

them up and took them to Dutch New Guinea. Later they were sent to Australia for hospital care and finally home to San Francisco on Nov. 6.

"It's great to be home," he said, "but I still can't seem to get enough to eat. Yes, I really swell—I eat all the time."

Japs Fire on Men Trapped in Ship

NEW YORK, Oct. 22 (A.A.P.).—Japanese guards deliberately fired on Americans who trapped in the hold of a sinking ship, were endeavouring to escape, says an announcement issued from General MacArthur's headquarters.

The ship—a Japanese transport—had been torpedoed by an American submarine, says the Associated Press correspondent at MacArthur's Headquarters.

It has been revealed that 5 American officers and men who had been prisoners in the Philippines for 2½ years, were rescued and are safe in New Guinea," the correspondent continues.

"All are in good condition except five men, who are recovering from bullet and grenade wounds.

"These men were among those Jap prisoners who were being shipped northwards on the Japanese transport.

"Others who escaped from the transport were hunted down and killed as they swam. Some who reached the beach were executed by the Japanese.

"Filipino guerillas cared for the 83 survivors until they were picked up and taken south by submarine and planes. Three Americans were found dead from stab wounds on the beach. Two had their hands tied behind their backs.

"A large number of Americans went down with the ship. Japanese losses were also heavy.

"Lieutenant Richard Cook and Staff Sergeant Joseph Cole elected to remain with the Filipino guerillas.

Inhuman Treatment

"The Americans had been prisoners in the Davao penal camp since the fall of Bataan and Corregidor.

"The commandant of the prison ordered a large group last February to work on an airfield. They were housed in four little shacks.

"For the first two months they received 500 grammes of rice daily but by August the amount had been reduced to 3 grammes (one-tenth of 1b.).

"In addition they received squash, also a water reed called yaqing, a little fish and no limited quantities of salt.

"Despite the hard work in blazing sun, guards armed with clubs several times went about them to force them to do more work.

"After one alleged attempt escape the prisoners had their shoes taken from them, given the sharp pick and shovel work around stones, which badly cut their feet.

Horror Death Charge Denied By Jap General

March 16 1946

Manila (U)—Japanese Lt. Gen. Shiyoku Kuo, with hundreds of horror deaths formally charged against him by the prosecution, pleaded innocent today on arraignment before a United States war-crimes trial commission.

He was in charge of "supervision, transportation, welfare, custody and administration" of Allied prisoners during the last year of the Japanese administration of the Philippines, Chief Prosecutor Lt. Col. Frederick A. Baird, Baton Rouge, La., told the commission.

Prisoners Starved

Baird's 14-page indictment listed deliberate starvation of prisoners; pilfering of Red Cross supplies; beatings — including among the victims Capt. (now Maj.) Arthur Wermuth, "One-Man Army" of Bataan; using prison camps as anti-aircraft gun sites, thus drawing Allied attacks; using prisoners to construct and maintain military installations; failure to mark prison camps or prison ships, and group punishments for individual offenses.

Climaxing the indictment, Baird described the hell-cruise of the Shinyo Maru—a trip that only 83 of the 750 prisoners aboard survived. Many suffocated, starved or died of disease in their 13 days afloat. Then the ship was torpedoed, and Japanese officers, said Baird, pursued in small boats the struggling prisoners still afloat, "killing and wounding as many as they could by gunfire and swords, and executing 36 who had been rescued by another Japanese ship."

Kuo, sweltering in wrinkled, patched Japanese army woolens, listened to the half-hour summary of atrocities and announced firmly:

"I am not guilty!"

News articles about the horrors suffered by the prisoners

Chapter 12

Return to Civilization

Perhaps because you have read the stories of Murray's captivity during World War II you would like to more know about his life since then. Shortly after he arrived home, in fact in only a month, we were married. We were supposed to have several weeks of Rest & Relaxation, but two weeks after we were married he had to turn in to the hospital with a bout of hookworm. After recovery we went to the Redistribution Station where Murray's records, including financial and medical status, were brought up to date.

He was then assigned to Minter Field in Bakersfield for refresher pilot training. In May of 1945 he was given the choice of going to Command & General Staff School in Leavenworth, Kansas or the Intelligence School in Florida. After giving it consideration, Murray decided on the former. While in Kansas a letter was forwarded saying that he had enough points to be discharged honorably. The course in Kansas was six weeks, and we returned to Minter Field around August. It was planned that Murray would be discharged in October.

After discharge Murray felt it was time to go back to University to finish his Bachelor's Degree. His sister was going to USC, and because of the GI Bill he was able to enroll at that school. He needed units in English so he took a course in Religion as Literature. This course, along with his rescue and former upbringing, got him interested in going into the ministry. While he was still going to school he taught a Sunday School class of adults and also went to various churches to talk to youth groups.

In June of 1946 we had a wonderful baby boy. When our son was ten months old Murray had pneumonia and had to go again to a Veterans' Hospital. When he had almost recovered he had a relapse. He eventually recovered and got his Bachelor's Degree. He then made up his mind to go to work. In 1949 we had a daughter and in 1951 we moved from Eagle Rock to Burbank, California. We had another daughter in 1962. Murray's mother died at the age of 90 and his dad six months later at age 95. As they lived not too far from us in Glendale we were able to help them take care of each other in their home.

After several jobs Murray went back to his first love, Art, and entered the Art Center School of Design where he received another Bachelor's Degree. He worked several years for architectural firms such as Perreira & Luckman and Daniel, Mann, Johnson & Mendenhall. After some time he became his own boss and did freelance illustrations for many different architects.

Many people told Murray he had a special talent for teaching. Again he returned to school at UCLA and received his teaching credential.

His first school was Emerson Junior High in Westwood, where he had done his practice teaching. Besides teaching art, he taught some remedial reading as he had a general credential. Although most of his pupils were from families highly motivated to learn, he had to travel 25 miles each way to our home in Burbank so he requested a transfer to a San Fernando Valley school. He then became a teacher at Olive Vista Junior High School in Sylmar. Murray taught for at least 19 years and retired at the age of 65 in 1985.

He made slide shows of his students' art work with narration and music. His students made tie-dye banners as well as crayon resist and ink projects.

Murray thought when he went into teaching he would have more time to paint watercolors for himself. This didn't happen because he was so conscientious in preparing assignments as well as grading fairly. He has made many friends of teachers and students who are still family friends. The last three years he taught English as a Second Language because another teacher needed Art to be able to teach, and Murray's minor was in language.

In 1969 and 1971 we traveled to Mexico in a VW camper during the summer for a period of five or six weeks. His purpose was to become fluent in Spanish.

The year we retired our children gave us airline tickets to Great Britain. Because our heritage is English and Scottish we visited Edinburgh and planned to visit Alt Bay, where his grandparents lived. We only got as far as Inverness.

In 1987 my mother came to live with us. We had plans to move to Bishop where our oldest daughter and her family lived, and Murray hoped to continue his painting of landscapes in the beautiful surrounding countryside. Three years later my mother said we should go on with our lives and we did move to Bishop in June 1990.

From 1985 to 1997 Murray did get to paint many watercolors. He also designed banners for our church in Burbank and also in Bishop.

Murray belonged to Burbank Art Association and The Valley Watercolor Association as well as the Society of Illustrators. He won many ribbons and sold many paintings. He also designed a logo for the Survivors of *Shinyo Maru* reunion which was made into patches, and a plaque dedicated to the Andersonville Historic Site in Andersonville, Georgia where he also gave the Invocation.

Murray spoke at memorial services for churches, Rotary Clubs and Lions Clubs, as well as for high school classes. Murray tried to keep physically fit by exercising and eating right—no fat, no sugar, and no salt. He loved to walk, hike and take pictures. He loved music and after attempting to play the guitar and bag-pipes he tried to play harmonica, particularly "blues." He loved to eat all varieties of ethnic foods as well as popcorn and ice cream. He loved people and he loved life. He was my sweetheart, my friend, a loving husband, father, and grandfather.

Murray with a few of the survivors at the 50ᵗʰ Anniversary

LIST OF EVACUEES FROM THE PHILIPPINE ISLANDS

NAME	RANK	BRANCH	SERIAL NO.	HOME ADDRESS
McGee, John H.	Col.	Inf.	018600	Minot, North Dakota
Chenoweth, Wm. C.	Lt. Col.	CE	020621	1243 Cherokee Road Louisville, Ky. Highland 5616
Fischer, Harry O.	Lt. Col.	CE	0260832	422 E. Huisache Ave., San Antonio, Texas. P22031
Blakeslee, Robert B.	Major	Ord.	0334461	18 Catherine Street, South Glens Falls, N.
Shoss, Morris L.	Major	CAC	022973	2627 Oakdale Street, Houston, Texas.
Cain, William P.	Capt.	Inf.	0310076	3631 Monroe Street, Columbia, S. C.
Dale, Eugene P.	Capt.	AC	0421898	612 N. Grand Ave., Enid, Oklahoma. Enid 1913
Donlon, James D.	Capt.	FA	0325720	900 C Street Antioch, California.
Gallagher, Frederick J.	Capt.	CE	0890515	950 N. 6th Ave., Tucson, Arizona.
Gillespie, John P.	Capt.	AC	0386395	377 W. Jackson Street Sigourney, Iowa.
Morrett, John J.	Capt.	FA	0375500	1320 E. High Street Springfield, Ohio.
Pflueger, Theodore L.	Capt.	CE	0372888	Hebron, Nebraska.
Playter, John C.	Capt.	FA	0375952	2126 N. Park Street, Joplin, Missouri.5168
Schwarz, Bert	Capt.	AC	0420648	210 W. 90th Street, New York, New York. Schuyler 4-9183
Steinhauser, Charles A.	Capt.	AC	0286284	304 G Avenue, Seaside, Oregon.
Denson, Harvey T.	1st Lt.	AC	0401146	Granger, Texas.
Johnson, Ralph R., Jr.	1st Lt.	AC	0419953	315A West Queen St., Inglewood, Calif. Orchard 70352

List of evacuees from the Philippine Islands

NAME	RANK	BRANCH	SERIAL NO.	HOME ADDRESS
LeClear, Francis E.	1st Lt	CAC	0393420	701 Ionia, Lansing, Michigan.
Sharp, Felix C., Jr.	1st Lt	CAC	0395703	2825 Oak Street, Jacksonville, Fla.
Skinner, Harry J.	1st Lt	Inf.	0890440	2708 Grove Street, Berkeley, Calif. Berk. 1242
Sneddon, Murray M.	1st Lt	AC	0407072	653 Glenoaks Blvd., Glendale, Calif.
Snowden, Paul S.	1st Lt	Inf.	0890512	1036 East Jackson St. Sapulpa, Oklahoma.
Tresniewski, Edward S.	1st Lt	Inf.	0890334	109 Saratoga Street, Cohoes, New York.
Vann, James K.	1st Lt	Inf.	0890264	Winona, Missouri.
Robinett, George R.	2nd Lt	AC	0928862	25 No. Polk Street, Eugene, Oregon.
Gillin, Donald F.	M/Sgt	AC	19049419	626 E. Palmer Ave., Glendale, Calif. Citrus 1-2093
Johnstone, Charles C.	T/Sgt	Inf.	6281701	1316 112th W St., Cleveland, Ohio.
Kuskie, Glen E.	T/Sgt	Inf.	20739039	6660 Gaviota Ave., Long Beach, Calif. 2-4947
McClure, Cecil H.	T/Sgt	AC ✓	6288045	1242 Marfa Ave., Dallas, Texas.
Bolitho, Hayes H.	S/Sgt	AC ✓	19054572	525 W. Diamond St., Butte, Montana. 2-4113
Haskell, Willard L.	S/Sgt	Sig. C.	11011290	Chachapacassett Rd., Barrington, R. I. Warren 656R
Kirker, Robert J.	S/Sgt	AC ✓	19012609	Paradise California.
Donohoe, Jack M.	Sgt	AC ✓	19000221	779 W. 5th Street, Reno, Nevada.
Granz, Donald James	Sgt	AC ✓	19048389	3530 Huntington Blvd. Fresno, Calif.

- 2 -

List of evacuees from the Philippine Islands

Bier, Jesse	T/3	Med.	11017163	38 Dartmouth Street, Lawrence, Mass.
Billick, Ray E.	T/3	AC ✓	6913614	Box 44, Nampa, Idaho. 689 J.
Booth, John W.	T/3	QM	19038334	Perham, Minn.
Golino, Peter J.	T/3	AC ✓	6913868	603 E. Green, Gallup, N. Mexico.
Greene, James R.	T/3	AC ✓	19045769	Altamont, Illinois, Box 24.
McComas, James F.	T/3	Armored (Inf.)	20700201	201 - 3rd Avenue, NE, Brainard, Minn.
McPherson, Donald I.	T/3	AC ✓	6932512	709 North 28th St., Lincoln, Nebraska.
Rose, Denver R.	T/3	(CAC)	17010471	c/o General Delivery, Houston, Texas.
Radcliff, Otis E.	T/3	(CAC)	6897340	Scotland Neck, N. C.
Wilson, Harold W.	T/3	CE	35014165	Nutwood, Ohio.
Bennett, John R.	T/4	Ord.	12032451	Henry Street, Hempstead, L.I., N.Y.
Biddle, William E.	T/4	Armored (Inf.)	15061445	1028 So. 16th St., Vincennes, Ind.
Browning, Paul L.	T/4	AC ✓	19017601	931 L Street, Centralia, Washington
Frederick, William T.	T/4	AC ✓	19056741	P.O. Box 83, Ojar, California.
Horabin, William S.	T/4	CAC	20842353	Route #4, Box 627, Albuquerque, New Mex.
Hughes, Roy S.	T/4	AC ✓	17016510	2620 Armand Place, St. Louis, Missouri.
Knudson, Lyle G.	T/4	AC ✓	19010193	2823 Malan Avenue, Ogden, Utah.
Latham, Calvin E.	T/4	Med.	19013454	Rexburg, Idaho, R.F.D. #3.

- 3 -

List of evacuees from the Philippine Islands

NAME	RANK	BRANCH	SERIAL NO.	HOME ADDRESS
Lorton, Bill J.	T/4	AC ✔	6574554	1540 So. 2nd East St. Salt Lake City, Utah.
Motsinger, E. A.	T/4	Inf	6280340	Box 444, Webb City, Mo.
Overton, Cletis O.	T/4	AC ✔	17010094	Rolla, Arkansas, Route #1.
Parker, Buster	T/4	QM	6583121	Clear Creek, West Virginia.
Simkins, Marcus N.	T/4	Med.	18017464	Route #1, Buda, Texas.
Stymelski, John	T/4	Inf	6832358	23465 Mackay, Hamtramick, Michigan.
Caputo, Marco A.	T/5	CE	32092484	23 Taylor Street, Ft. Edward, New York.
Hagins, Isaac B.	T/5	AC ✔	7022245	Freeport, Penn.
Hoctor, Francis	T/5	AC ✔	11010371	26 Western Avenue, Bidderford, Mass.
Ingley, Lawrence P.	T/5	Ord.	19002307	Route 6, Lubbock, Texas.
Jones, Joseph H.	T/5	Ord.	35032427	Oak Hill, Ohio, R.F.D. #4.
Mackowski, John J.	T/5	CE	32109397	652 Leonard St., Brooklyn, N.Y.
Moore, Lewis A.	T/5	CAC	6967765	Glencoe, Alabama.
Olinger, D. J.	T/5	CAC	19056665	143 Steele Street, Denver, Colorado.
Tipton, Lawrence	T/5	CAC	15065729	1310 E. Herman Ave., Dayton, Ohio.
Gardner, Walter E.	Cpl	AC ✔	12026548	P.O. Box 294, Hopewell, Virginia. Hopewell 3133
Lamkin, Joseph P.	S/Sgt	Inf	20700241	Proctor, Minnesota.
Schoenborne, Omar A.	S/Sgt	Ord	19052508	Chippewa Indian Agency, Cass Lake, Minnesota.

- 4 -

List of evacuees from the Philippine Islands

Remembrance

I thank my God upon every remembrance of you. (Philippians 1:3)
I want you to know you are never forgotten;
That the old, old days hid in memory sweet
Are still a part of my life that I cherish—
Without them so much would be incomplete.
And you are mixed up with so much I remember,
Your name so often I utter in prayer;
Never forgotten, on earth or in heaven,
Always the child of God's tenderest care.
I want you to know you are never forgotten,
That my thoughts and my prayers are folding you round.
Rest in His promises, go where He sends you,
Do what He bids you, faithful be found.
Look up and trust Him, a new year is dawning,
Stretch out your hand and take His today;
Bought by Him, loved by Him, never forgotten,
Hid in His heart forever and aye.

This poem was read at the dispersal of Murray's ashes on July 4, 1998, near Loch Leven after a three-hour hike from North Lake. Those present were Fiona Sneddon, Tom Sneddon, Fawnn Sneddon, Hank & Bennett Sneddon, Wendy & Joe Duncan, Jesse & Matt Duncan and Laurie Reber & Samantha & Beau Reber. It took three hours crossing the creek in two places and going through at least ten snow banks of varying degrees of difficulty to arrive at a beautiful spot where we decided to go no farther due to the next snow bank.

About the Author

Murray Sneddon was born in Canada, but lived in California from the age of 4. After attending UCLA and taking art classes, he decided that joining the Army Air Corps would be much more exciting.

After training, he was shipped to the Philippines where he worked as a reconnaissance pilot with the 2nd Observation Squadron flying single-engine Thomas Morris biplanes. Japanese bombs destroyed their airfield, so they were sent to Manila and then to Bataan. There, the American forces were forced to surrender, and Sneddon became a POW. This began his 2 years of living hell; which began with the Bataan Death March, and ended more than 2 years later with a narrow escape from the sinking Shinyo Maru. He was finally rescued by the submarine Narwhal, and began his journey back home to his family and his sweetheart, Fiona, whom the thought of had given him the courage and strength to live through all of the atrocities he witnessed.

After his arrival back home in the States, he married Fiona, and was awarded a honorable discharge shortly afterward. He then returned to college at USC on the GI Bill where he earned his Bachelor's Degree. After working at several jobs, Murray returned to his first love, art, and earned another Bachelor's Degree from the Art Center School of Design. He worked for an architectural firm and later did freelance illustrations. He went back to school again and earned his teaching credential and taught junior high art for 19 years.

He continued his work in art and design, and became a public speaker. He and his wife had 3 children, daughters Laurie and Wendy and son Tom. He died of leukemia before this book was totally finished, leaving behind many friends and family members who will always remember his love for life and his courage.